A Gift of Love

The first
hundred
years of
The Lutheran
Home at Topton
1896-1996

TOPTON

*by
David A.
Miller, II*

Printed by
The Kutztown Publishing Co., Inc.

ISBN 0-9648388-0-X

Printed in the United States of America

DEDICATION

This history is dedicated to all of the members of the Alumni Association of The Lutheran Home at Topton. They comprise the 1,618 orphans taken in beginning May 17, 1897. Most of them spent their entire childhood here, learning valuable life lessons while they were cared for with Christian love.

They left "the hill" as young adults and have had fine careers, raised their families and struggled with life's challenges as we all do.

While The Lutheran Home at Topton has now broadened its outlook into services for the elderly and community services, it began its existence as The Lutheran Orphans Home, with a specific mission to care for these "orphans and half-orphans."

On the event of the 100th anniversary of this proud organization, we therefore humbly dedicate this book to the members of the Alumni Associaton.

ACKNOWLEDGMENTS

To Rev. Heilman, Rev. Raker, Rev. Holter, Rev. Henry, Rev. Reinert and Rev. Buehrle: I am in awe of all of you. It's been a joy to work personally with both Rev. Reinert and Rev. Buehrle.

To the multitude of faithful chroniclers of histories going back over a hundred years; we have never met you, but we do appreciate your care in keeping the memories.

To the Alumni Association, whose help made this whole project possible.

To Lona Farr, Vice President, Institutional Advancement, for her trust and faith.

To those we interviewed:

. Pat Gieroczynski, R.N. *Coordinator, Special Care Unit*

. Amy Reinsel, *Director of Managed Care Services*

. Dorthie Kaylor, *Director of Admissions*

. Nancy Henry Kline

(granddaughter of Rev. J. O. Henry)

. Terry A. Lieb, *Director of Family Life Services Dept.*

I wish we had enough pages for all your fascinating information!

To the entire Lutheran Home Public Relations Department, with special kudos to Doris Kahle, Director of Media/Community Relations, for her organizational help par excellence, and to Barbara Schroeder for photographic research and editing.

A special 'thank you' to interning Rebecca Seerveld.

To my wife Emily, for even more than her usual patience and understanding!

CONTENTS

FOREWORD

To comfort and to bless,

To find a balm for woe,

To tend the lone and fatherless,

Is angels work below.

This is the Spirit of the religion of Jesus Christ. It finds its motive not only in what He has commanded, but also in what He did.

When He commissioned the twelve apostles, He not only commanded them to preach the message of the Kingdom, but said unto them: "Heal the sick, cleanse the lepers, raise the dead. Freely have ye received — freely give."

Where do ideas begin? Did the idea for The Lutheran Home at Topton begin exactly 100 years ago? Of course not. How far back can we trace this 'golden thread' of caring for orphans in the history of our church?

Early in our church's history, in the days of the Apostles, contributions for the relief of the needy, especially the widows and orphans, were sent to Jerusalem to be distributed.

Let's travel to Germany in the late 1600's. Our journey leads us to August Herman Francke, Theologian and Philanthropist. He was a Pietist of the School of Spencer, in full accord with the doctrines of the Lutheran Church and was an intimate and cherished friend of Spencer.

Possessed of a fiery zeal, together with his piety and a superb organizational ability, he began his work among the poor of Halle, Germany. Francke started with a one-room school for the poor in 1695 with just seven guilders and built the first Lutheran Orphan Asylum in 1698.

Within a year, this single room was found insufficient and others were added. This was the beginning of the famous Halle Orphan House, which with Divine blessing, developed into a series of institutions and has accomplished a great work.

Other buildings were added, until a regular village of educational and benevolent institutions emerged. At the time of Francke's death, thousands had been helped.

Astoundingly, August Herman Francke never asked anyone for money for ANY of his numerous enterprises. He implicitly trusted God as the supply of the means necessary to carry on his work. A grand beginning.

Now, follow this concept to England two hundred years later. It is reported for us in the <u>Orphans' Home Paper</u>, Sept. 1901.

> **Sept. 1901: The Rev. George Muller, the great Orphan Home man of England, was a unique character. He gives a birds-eye view of the Orphans' Homes erected by him without ever asking for a penny. He was born in Kroppenstadt, Prussia, Germany. His father wanted his son to become a minister, simply so he would have an easy life.*
>
> *At the University of Halle, Muller "served Satan, but never neglected communion." He was ordained as a Lutheran minister and received a call as a Jewish missionary to England.*
>
> *He started a mission near Bristol and came across a book entitled "The Life of August Herman Franke, the Great Orphans' Home Man of Germany."*
>
> *He states that in 1826, August H. Franke spoke to his soul. From this time on, he trusted or looked to the*

----

*Editor's Note: When you see the indented, italicized paragraphs throughout the book, you'll know that we're quoting from <u>The Orphans' Home Paper</u> *or* <u>The Herald</u>.

*Lord, like Franke, for everything. The Lord never
forsook him. As a sample to show the people how God
cared for those who trusted in Him alone, he started an
Orphans' home on a small scale. He asked for and
received small, then large sums, received as a direct
answer to prayer.*

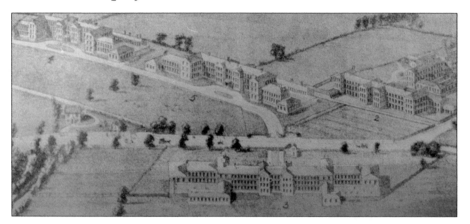

*In this cut, you see where over 2,000 children are
clothed, fed and educated. He never received one cent's
worth of provisions on credit and never went into debt.
When a new building was to be put up, he prayed until
he had all the money needed before he started.*

Life in Europe was punctuated by a seemingly unending
series of wars. The Germans knew all too well about orphans
and, out of necessity, had been dealing with that problem for
many generations.

Because of this and other devastating situations, thousands
of German Lutherans started coming to these shores in the
1700's, primarily through the port of Philadelphia.

They came (of course) to the 'Germantown' section, then
moved their families to the rich, rolling lands of Berks and
Lehigh Counties. The gently rolling hillsides and valleys
reminded them of their homeland in the old country.

They were proud to be "Pennsilfannisch Deitsch" (Pennsylvania German.) If you couldn't make out the dialect, it
sounded like they said "Pennsylvania Dutch."

By 1730, the Lutheran Church was growing so rapidly that it was impossible to find enough pastors to supply the new congregations. A subsequent appeal to Germany for money and pastoral help was one of the most important actions in the Church's history. The year was 1742.

Henry Melchior Muhlenberg

Dr. Muhlenberg visited the Tulpehocken Congregation in western Berks County the following year and, in 1745, married Anna Marie, the oldest daughter of Conrad Weiser.

Weiser, a churchman, counsellor, soldier and Indian interpreter, wrote an important page in American history. Following his marriage to Weiser's daughter, the life of Muhlenberg, the Patriarch of the Lutheran Church in America, became inseparably linked with Berks County.

Within 25 years after the Revolutionary War, almost every Lutheran congregation in the county erected a new church. A number of these beautiful edifices are still standing and have vital, active congregations.

One pastor, John Andrew Schulze, was elected to the State Legislature. He was Governor of Pennsylvania from 1823-1829. Pastor Peter Filbert became Reading's first Mayor in 1847.

The great stream of Lutheran immigration in the 18th and 19th centuries also contributed to the growth of the church. The pastors and people of this valley, taking all into consideration, have felt that we should have an Orphanage somewhere in these parts.

In 1897, there were over 122,000 confirmed members in the Synod, comprising all of eastern Pennsylvania, half of New Jersey and parts of Delaware and Maryland. This large and wealthy Synod had, thus far, only the

Germantown Orphans' Home (with room for about 80 children) to shelter, feed, clothe and instruct its poor orphans. It had been established in 1859.

In the rationale for another facility for orphans, it was pointed out that:

· The Germantown home was 'unfortunately situated' for our people, difficult and expensive to visit. · The Germantown Home took children ONLY if their fathers were dead; no provision for any other option.

· Others were rising to the need: The Catholic Orphans' Home in Reading, the Home for Friendless Children, etc.

· Lutheran Stronghold: The Lutherans are particularly strong and numerous in the Counties of Berks and Lehigh.

· No county in our whole Synod (not even excepting Philadelphia), has as many Lutherans in it as does Berks County.

· There is no district in the whole eastern United States (and perhaps not in the western part), in which the Lutherans are as strong as between Reading and Allentown. This is Lutheran territory, the heart of our Synod.

· The property in Berks Co. is valued at over $80,000,000. Since half of the people in Berks Co., are Lutherans, it is safe to say that at least $30,000,000 worth of this property is owned by Lutherans. The people of Berks Co. are also reported to have over $17,000,000 on interest.

Looking at all of this, it is safe to say that the Lutherans of Berks are able to erect an Orphans' Home at Topton. We are also very confident that they are willing to erect that Home, as soon as they fully understand what we are about to do.

These excerpts from Vol. 1, No. 1 of the <u>Orphans' Home Paper</u> mirror the feelings voiced at the Conference Sunday-School Convention, held at Boyertown on October 16, 1894.

Let's take a brief look at early traditions of child care and family life in the 'colonies.' Childhood was short, not only because children worked early, but also because it was so often ended abruptly by death.

In New England, in the 17th century in relatively healthy areas, one in ten infants died before their first birthday; in unhealthy areas, the rate was three in ten. Today it is less than one in 100.

ORPHANAGES IN THE U.S.

The first orphanage in this country owed its existence to seven Ursuline nuns in New Orleans in 1798. Only 15 other privately supported orphanages were founded between 1800 and 1830. Then, public and private organizations, dissatisfied with the almshouse solution, launched an optimistic orphanage boom.

By 1850, New York State alone had 27 asylums. Though it's hard to believe today, orphanages were widely hailed as ideal institutions in the mid-19th century.

THE ORPHAN TRAINS

In a mass displacement rivaled only by the Children's Crusade of the 13th century, more than 200,000 orphaned, neglected and abandoned children were transported from the crowded, filthy streets of New York and the eastern cities to the salubrious air of the midwestern countryside in the 75 years between 1854 and 1929.

Most of them were in the care of New York's Children's Aid Society, which characterized itself as the first organization in this country dedicated to improving the living conditions of children.

Charles Loring Brace, an innovative, idealistic minister turned social worker, founded the society in 1853. He was convinced that institutional life (or life on the squalid streets) turned poor children into adults who were likely to be either a danger or a burden to society.

Instead of orphanages, Brace proposed "the family as God's Reformatory" and sent the children first to nearby farms in New Jersey and New York and then west on trains that were then making the wide-open spaces accessible. Children were gathered from orphanages and other institutions as well as the streets, and some were delivered to the society's doorstep by distraught parents who could not care for them.

From its beginning, the Orphan Train movement was considered cruel and underhanded by some--tearing children from their families, converting Catholics to Protestants, contaminating the countryside with New York's young criminals--and brilliant and humane by others, who saw it as a precursor of today's foster care.

Institutions grew as the population increased; first dreadful almshouses, then orphanages that separated children from indigent adults and were hailed as "ideal."

However, by the first third of this century, as is shown in our own Home's history, orphanages fell from being perceived as "the perfect institution" to something less. Within a decade, they were being discarded in favor of foster care.

APPRENTICESHIP

Apprenticeship for both rich and poor had a long history in the mother country, beginning in the Middle Ages. In the sixteenth century, English parents who could not provide proper training for their children were required to apprentice them to a trade, thus keeping them from wandering from place to place and becoming dissolute.

Colonial apprenticeship was, in addition to being a standard 'job training' method, an early form of foster care. This was particularly true for poor young children whose families could not provide for them.

The ancient institution of the extended family also served the migrants and immigrants as a way to care for children whose parents could not. Sections of cities became ethnic magnets, such as "Little Italy."

In the big cities, families lived within a few doors or blocks of each other. Out in the country, the farm family was, by definition, isolated and self-sufficient. That is, unless some disaster happened to a parent.

While the care of orphans is far from the entire history of The Lutheran Home at Topton, it is where the history begins and much of its strong reputation was made.

Our next destination is St. John's Lutheran Church in Boyertown, PA. This beautiful edifice still stands, proudly serving its present congregation.

However, inside these same walls, there was a gathering in 1894, where a vital question was presented. Let's continue our journey.

Chapter 1

"WHAT CAN BE DONE...?"

L ove is a mystery. A 100-year gift of love is an even more wonderful mystery! This gift of love, The Lutheran Home at Topton, began with love. Our story begins with a question...but it does NOT begin in Topton.

The fascinating mystery starts with the first Berks County Sunday School Convention, Oct. 16, 1894 held at St. John's Lutheran Church in Boyertown. Someone, obviously guided by love, put this question in the suggestion box.

> **"What can be done on behalf of the orphans of our congregations or Sunday Schools being deprived of their homes and means of Christian education?"**

We have no videotape. No instant replay. Nor do we have a real understanding of life a century ago. By our standards, virtually every child is born healthy. We now live into our 80's, 90's and longer. This is the reality of health in the 1990's.

Think back a century. What do we know about those times? We know that the family, the church and the local community formed the backbone of life. Travel was difficult, although the shining steel ribbons of the railroads had knit the new country together. (A town NEEDED train service to prosper.)

How did people live back then? Towns were small. You KNEW your neighbors. The family farm was representative of a large portion of the population. Inside plumbing? Maybe. Electricity? Maybe. A car? Probably not. Air conditioning? Forget it.

We know that life was much harder (usually much shorter.) Couples had a lot more children. Many of them died. Here is an example, representative of the records we have examined for this book.

It is late winter of 1894. It started cold, and it has stayed bitter cold. But there is cold much worse than ice. You are a young Pennsylvania Dutch farmer, sitting on the edge of your bed, trying to hold back the great racking sobs. Hot tears run down into your beard. You have just returned from the cemetery.

Your young wife has died in childbirth. Oh, this is impossible! Yet, part of you <u>knows</u> it is true. Inside is an emptiness as hollow and as deep as a well. It strikes terror into your bones. You look down and see that you have been rubbing your rough hands together over and over, as if you could wash away the memory of her death.

You pat the place where she slept, to call her back...so everything would be all right again. The winter sun slants in, lighting the quilt she made. But there is no warmth in the sunlight and only ice in your heart.

You hear the sounds of your two young boys, running around in the kitchen, being 'shushed' by the relatives. They aren't sure what is going on, but they love the attention! From time to time, your sister opens the door a crack to check on you. You try to speak, but only a croak comes out. She lowers her eyes, closes the door. She is all cried out.

You are devastated. It is impossible to think. Your whole world was this small farm, your wife and your two little boys. This morning, you buried your young wife and baby girl.

What on earth can you do? What will happen now?

Can you put yourself into that young father's place? You've just buried your young wife. All you have left is your farm and your two little boys, and you KNOW that you cannot take care of them AND run the farm. What on earth can you do?

Let's go back to Boyertown. The convention is drawing to a close. All the questions from the suggestion box are being read aloud. Picture the whispers and nods when <u>this</u> question is read. There is much discussion, then the announcement that lunch is being served downstairs.

See the ministers walking together in their black suits and starched collars, hands clasped behind the back (or gesturing to make a point.) While it is a warm October afternoon, they don't seem to notice the brilliant colors of the autumn leaves. They are in deep discussion on this troubling question.

It certainly must have 'hit a nerve' in almost every congregation. A committee was formed to study the problem, made up of Rev. M. C. Horine, D.D.; Rev. J. J. Kuendig, D.D.; Mr. H. W. Schick, and Mr. A. Bendel, all of Reading. The following April, they reported to the Reading Conference.

Their report sings in a solemn and formal style no longer used. Read it out loud to get a feel of the faith and love these good Lutherans felt. (We've found the actual piece of tablet paper used for the report. It's reprinted, crossed out words and all!)

Reading, Pa. Feb. 11th, 1895.

To the Officers and Members of the ~~Synod County~~ Reading Conference.

We the undersigned committee appointed by the Sunday School Convention held at Boyertown on Oct. 16th 1894 to consider and present to your honorable body the following ~~question submitted~~ to said convention "What could be done on behalf of the orphans of our congregations who have been deprived of their homes and Christian education" have after deliberate consideration arrived at the following.

That in view of the fact that the Germantown Orphans Home can only accommodate the orphans of Philadelphia and adjacent districts and only receive whole orphans and we in this large populated district have a number of orphans in orphan houses of other denomination who are very active in securing our orphans especially the Catholic Church, we deem it advisable to take steps towards providing for the ~~homeless~~ orphans and half-orphans of our congregations. ~~who are homeless.~~

We as a committee would recommend that we commence in a small manner and in good faith, towards providing for them, and feel satisfied that God will provide as needs require, and also that a committee be appointed to take up this work.

Submitting the above for your kind consideration, we remain

Yours respectfully.

M. C. Horine
J. J. Kuendig.
Henry W. Schick
A. Bendel

3

> "We deem it advisable to take steps toward providing for the homeless orphans and half orphans of our congregations. We would recommend that we commence in a small manner and in good faith towards providing for them, and feel quite satisfied that God will provide as needs require; and also that a committee be appointed to take up this work."

Before we truly begin at the beginning...let's look back from today...the <u>end</u> of the first hundred years. The Lutheran Home at Topton has been born and reborn AT LEAST three times (so far.) Its life is like a growing spiral. We'll be examining these phases in detail.

We will see that, if an organization doesn't grow and 'recreate itself' somehow, it will die.

The Lutheran Home is quite healthy, thank you. The reasons WHY are what this 100-year history is all about.

We have been given enough perspective to see the hand of love guiding this amazing creation for its first hundred years.

Now, let's go back in time and look with the eyes of love.

St. John's Lutheran Church, Boyertown, PA (as church looked in 1894) Exterior (left) Sunday School Room (right)

Getting Synod approval gets things rolling! The committee recommended that "we commence." The conference agreed that the report should be presented to the Synod. On June 11, 1895, they said, "The Reading Conference feels the necessity for establishing in this strongly Lutheran section, a home for orphans; **friendless, homeless and neglected** children. It asks that the Synod approve these intentions."

You may have noted the heart-breaking adjectives. **It strikes us that anyone with objections would have been hard pressed to speak up.** We note that the Synod DID approve the committee's recommendations quickly and heartily.

The following May, a provisional constitution was adopted and a Board of Trustees was elected by the Reading conference. This Board was given the authority to purchase a farm and establish the Home. First officers were: Rev. U. P. Heilman, President; the omnipresent H. W. Schick, Secretary and E. S. Wertz, Treasurer.

The new institution was granted a charter as "The Lutheran Orphans' Home in Berks County, Pennsylvania." Rev. Heilman, a strong and able leader, was elected Superintendent. As we will see, the story of the early years of the Home is the record of <u>his</u> sincerity, patience, faith and stamina.

The new Trustees now had a dream. It had a name. It had a charter. However, it didn't exist. No matter. They would find it. Think back to the countryside 100 years ago. Mostly 'horse and buggy'

transportation. Few automobiles. Roads? The 'main roads' were passable, but side roads were poor.

It must have been exciting to be part of THAT committee, as they traveled through the fine, lush farmland, considering which property would be the "right one." There were more than 40 farms on the original list, all to be personally examined. Note that this was 'big news' in the area, and many of the towns made generous offers of money, labor, etc. This was true of Kutztown, Hamburg, Topton, among others.

Then they were down to six, centered around the Kutztown-Lyons-Topton area. Many of the farms offered excellent features. It was a difficult decision.

These were practical men. It made good sense to pick a spot near the center of the Synod. They wrote: " We are locating the Home not for this generation, but for many generations." Imagine the tingle they must have felt as they climbed the hill above Topton.

The town was given its name because it was the highest point in the railroad run from Philadelphia to Reading, hence they were truly at the TOP.

This was the Peter Diener farm, overlooking Topton and the fine farmland below. "It affords a grand view to the east, west and north of Topton. The farm contains about 105 acres and cost $7,000.00. There are at least 70 tillable acres; the rest is woodland and meadow. The farm contains never-failing springs in the woodland, which springs are high enough to run the water into the buildings."

It was purchased on Oct. 12, 1896, less than two years since the question was put in the collection box.

On Dec. 7, 1896, a charter was granted by the Berks County Court and "The Lutheran Orphans' Home in Berks County, Pennsylvania" was legally established. Just think how quick that process was, with no faxes, cellular phones or teleconferencing.

As we see how quickly and smoothly this process moved, we feel the gentle touch of the hand of love.

Chapter 2

THE EARLY YEARS

The Rev. Uriah P. Heilman, D.D.
1897-1900

We applaud the "search committee" (p. 5) for finding Rev. Uriah Peter Heilman to fill the job of the first Superintendent of "The Lutheran Orphans' Home in Berks County."

Put yourself in their shoes. You're interviewing Lutheran ministers, trying to get some of them interested in supervising something that doesn't even exist, has no congregation, no choir, no building.

Fortunately, they had Divine guidance and found Rev. Heilman. We might think that he started work when he moved into the farmhouse on the Peter Diener farm. Not so. Here was one very organized Superintendent. Besides

Mrs. Vesta Heilman
First Matron

Rev. Uriah P. Heilman
First Superintendent

the Orphanage, which included building it from the foundation up, there was a working farm to start...from scratch.

One of the most effective decisions he and the Board made was to publish immediately. The <u>Orphan's Home Paper</u> had its inaugural issue in January of 1897. Subscription was free, but it was announced that soon it would be 50c/year. Page 1 starts with a well-thought-out list of 'questions and answers.' Then follows a brief history, introduction of the Board of Trustees, and then the story of how the particular site was chosen.

Orphans' Home Paper.

Devoted in particular to the interests of the Evangelical Lutheran Orphans' Home of the Reading Conference, located at Topton, Pa., and in general to the interests of the poor and needy in our churches in Berks County.

He that hath pity upon the poor, lendeth unto the Lord; and that which he hath given will he pay him again. Prov. 19 : 17 ; 28 : 27.'

Edited by the Superintendent.   Published by the Board of Trustees.

All communications to this Paper should be addressed—Rev. U. P. Heilman, Athol, Berks Co., Pa.

ISSUED MONTHLY.   PRICE

Vol. I.   TOPTON, PA., JANUARY, 1897.   No. I.

Orphans' Home Paper ! *What kind of a paper is this?*

This is a paper which will tell you all about the new Orphans' Home the Lutherans in Berks County are about to build at Topton.

Yes, I heard they were going to build an Orphans' Home at Topton; but why do they want to build an Orphans' Home in Berks Co.?

This Paper will tell you all you desire to know about this. Please READ THIS PAPER THROUGH CAREFULLY.

So this Paper is to interest us in the new Orphans' Home. Has it anything else in view?

Yes; this Paper will also, in a general way, endeavor to interest you in all the poor, aged, helpless, afflicted and needy Lutherans in Berks County, and will seek to bring them some rays or hope and comfort.

Poor people! Poor orphans! Needy persons! Are there then any poor and needy persons in Berks County?

Yes, more than you think. Half the people in this world do not know how poor the other half is. Berks County is a wealthy county. Yet, as the Bible says, The poor we have always with us. Pastors and physicians see and hear what would

in works of love and charity,—yet, to break up the monotony, it will frequently contain other church information, especially concerning our own congregations in Berks county

Will this Paper come only in the English language?

This Paper cannot afford to come in two languages ; and since most of our people read English papers, this Paper comes in the English language. If any one cannot read English, let him command his son to read it and translate it to his parents ; this would be good and profitable exercise.

What does this Paper cost?

This Paper, for the present, costs you nothing. Read it carefully for several months and see how you like it. See what it has to say about *our* new Orphans' Home. Yes, say—*our* Orphans' Home.

There are in Berks Co. 30 Lutheran clergymen. 21 of these are in the active ministry. Of the rest, some are Professors, some are, at present, without a charge, aeral some are aged and have retired.   ugs.

There are in this county about 76 may, at eran congregations, and about 2˙ After the firmed Lutheran church member is to move, Besides these there are also in hans in his

Rev. Heilman wrote in a very DIRECT style. You don't have to wonder what he means. On page 5, he 'cuts to the chase' about the timetable for the new farm:

The farm buildings

We expect to begin farming in the Spring on our Topton farm. We need farm stock, yes the <u>entire</u> stock, for we have, as yet, nothing in that line; neither have we any money. All we have is faith and courage to ask.

Is there not a Lutheran in Berks who will bestow us a wagon? Another who will give us a plow? a harrow? a horse? a cow? a roller? a pig? harness?...We need also hay, oats and corn till we can harvest our own.

Whoever helps the Home along in any way, whether it is by a gift, or labor, etc. will get credit. Read, consider, RESOLVE, ACT!

A Gift of Love

Taking his own advice, page 8 is a FULL PAGE OF ADS!

Take a look at the wonderful outpouring of items from the congregations! It is as if they were just waiting for someone to give them a "wish list." Rev. Heilman knew these people well. They contributed everything from hens and chicks to four-horse wagons!

· *Feb. 1897: The Bernville congregation, through the influence of their pastor, Rev. J. J. Cressman, has promised to give us a brand new two-horse wagon, complete, with body and all.*

· *Mr. Wm. J. Harpel, Bernville agricultural dealer, has promised to give us a corn planter.*

· *Mr. D. C. Lotz, dealer in hardware and plows, 741 Penn St., Reading (see advertisement), is going to give us a plow.*

· *Messrs. Wise and Wise, of Amityville, are going to give us a good, strong new wheelbarrow. (Mr. Jacob Wise, wheelwright, is doing the wood work, and Mr. Urias Wise, blacksmith, is putting on the iron.)*

· *Mr. J. B. Bertoletle of Amity has promised us a pig.*

· *A gentleman from another county, who is interested in harnesses, asked me for the size and weight of one of our horses, stating that he would like to put a harness, free of charge, into our community.
Of course I accepted.*

· *From Stichter Hardware Co., 505 Penn St., Reading, - hay forks, 2 grain forks, 2 axes/handles, 2 hatchets, 3 shovels, 1 crow bar, 2 scythes, 2 manure forks.*

· *From Mr. Aaron B. Stein, of 948 Franklin St., Reading - 6 curry combs, 1 half-bushel measure, 6 rakes, 3 horse cards, 3 horse brushes, 1 grindstone with fixtures.*

· *From Mr. and Mrs. Isaac Weitzel, of Blandon, - 12 chickens. (Rev. Zweizig's)*

· *From Mr. Hiester Fisher, of Douglass township, - one shoat. (Rev. Heilman's)*

· *The Stouchsburg charge, Rev. A. Johnson Long, pastor, is getting ready for us a first class, No. 1 new four-horse wagon. This wagon is being built by the well known and extensive wagon building factory at Bernville, of which Mr. J. H. Rothermel, the proprietor, belongs to the Tulpehocken Lutheran congregation, near Bernville. In a later number we will state what each Sunday-school and congregation contributed toward this wagon. Mr. Rothermel himself contributes five dollars toward the two-horse wagon.*

· *Mr. N. S. Schmehl, of Trinity Church, Kutztown, has a one-horse cultivator ready for us. (Rev. Dr. Harkey's)*

· *Mr. Samuel Williams, of Spring Township (Kissinger's church), promises one plow with double and triple trees. (Rev. F. S. B.)*

· *Mr. Wm. Sheidy, of West Reading, has ready for us 6 chickens and one hen with brood.*

· *Geo. and Sarah Rebecca Sherk, children of Frank Sherk, of Spring Township (Kissinger's church), also promise 6 chickens and one hen with young. (Rev. Brownmiller)*

· *Miss Hannah Wertz, of Spring Township (Kissinger's church), will also give us chickens and a hen & chicks.*

· *The North Heidelberg congregation, Rev. J. J. Cressman, pastor, will present us with a spring harrow.*

· *Mr. Isaac D. Fegely, of Shamrock, has a grain drill ready for us, anytime we want it. (Rev. Kramlich's)*

Another plow was offered by a member of the Bernville congregation and another grain drill, but we had to inform the parties that we have plows and grain drills enough promised. See also promises for furniture in other parts of this Paper.

In the March, 1897 issue, Rev. Heilman is getting into high gear! The power of this little paper was astounding. He's asking for things that are needed within days...and knows that his readers will respond!

> *Moving time is coming. Is there not a farmer within several miles of Topton who will take a small (or large) load of straw to the barn on our Orphans' Farm, on or before the first of April? Another, who will haul a load of hay there? Another, who will take some corn fodder there? Another, who will put oats or corn there? We will not be there before April 1st, and when we do come, we need something to begin with. After we are started and settled we can help ourselves better.*

> *Mr. Jacob Fenstermaker, the man who lives on the farm now, says there is room in the barn for anything that is brought there; and he further states that he will help to unload hay, straw, & etc., that is brought there before he moves away.*

> ### WHAT WE YET NEED

> *To begin farming we yet need horses, cows, some pigs, four heavy farm harnesses, one double tree, hay, straw, feed cutter, a spike harrow, a roller, a horse hay rake; in short, everything one needs on a farm, except what is already reported that is promised.*

> *We have nothing. There is in the barn a stationary horse power, but some day we will need a threshing machine. The things donated do not all need to be quite new; we are also thankful for secondhand tools, implements, etc.*

> **We also take money that was used before.**

On March 30, 1897, Rev. Uriah Heilman and his wife, Alvesta, moved in to the farmhouse. (Most of the later histories call her Vesta, so we shall do the same.) They lost no time in preparing for their young charges.

Here's the account of that emotional day.

This is now an Orphans' Home in the full sense. Orphans, and poor orphans are actually here. May 17th, in the forenoon, the first children came to our door. They are fatherless and motherless, without means, and have had no regular home since their parents are dead. They were one here and one there. They came here to stay.

We welcomed them in, and I hope that we may be able to clothe, feed and educate them, and make this their permanent home till they are grown.

The orphans are: Sallie E. Carl, aged 6 yrs., and Clair E. Carl, almost 9 yrs. old. Their father and mother died in Kutztown, only two days apart of typhoid fever.

Sallie E. Carl and Clair E. Carl, the first orphans

While the day was beautiful, there were some sad and tearful eyes to be seen. The little orphans, of course, felt that coming here meant something serious and important for them, yet they could scarcely tell what it meant.

The little girl wept heartily when she came up the hill from Topton. Just before dinner, both the children could not contain themselves any longer and cried, without being able to tell why. So again in the evening when it began to grow dark outside. And so for several days, when they were not otherwise engaged, some sort of grief feeling of being forsaken overtook them. But they are happy now, and call this place home, and call us papa and mamma.

The sight of these homeless helpless orphans and their sighs and tears dearly affected the women in the home very much and made its impression upon the men. What brought us men to seriousness was the question

*whether we can take care of these little ones who fled to
us for refuge and shelter. Will the Lutherans in Berks
County give us money to fix up a home and resting
place for such little innocent wanderers? Why, of
course they will! They always said they would stand by
us, and I know they will.*

*A few weeks later, a visitor asked Sallie where she came
from. After a little study, she answered: "I came from
all over the world." She meant to say: Since my parents
died, I had no settled home, but was once here, once
there—everywhere. She was last near Allentown. Her
brother, Clair Carl, also had half a dozen stopping
places in this world since his parents died, and was last
at Boyertown.*

Orphans were "indentured." This ancient term means
that the agreement was originally written in duplicate on one
sheet of paper, then torn or cut apart irregularly, forming
indentations. One half was given to the master, the other to
the apprentice or family. The two parts fit together perfectly, making clear who was apprenticed to whom.

A site for the main building was selected and building
plans were made. The place chosen was at the prow of
the topmost hill. It's a grand view from the front porch
(and breathtaking from the bell-tower!)

The following brief story of the "groundbreaking" gives a
vivid picture of Rev. Heilman's character.

*On the 29th of June, 1897, in the morning at 6 o'clock,
the Superintendent, with pick and shovel on his back,
went out to the building site of the projected main
building and placed himself on the spot where his office
was to be. Turning towards sunrise, with folded hands
and uplifted face, he began, "In the name of the Father,
and of the Son, and of the Holy Ghost. Amen."*

*Then he dug out, in the shape of a cross, about the size
of a man, several wheelbarrowfuls of ground. Then
looking towards the north and kneeling in the cross-*

shaped opening, he offered a brief prayer, asking
God's choicest benediction upon the Home. In this
manner the ground for the Orphans' Home was
formally broken.

Years later, a writer says, "Some day, perhaps an inspired
artist will paint the picture of this indomitable man, silhou-
etted against the sky, as he kneels to pray in the cross-shaped
trench that he dug. The benediction that prayer evoked has
been the ever-firm foundation of the Home."

Perhaps it is not yet painted because too few have read
the story. Perhaps that writer's voice will **now** speak to a
reader of <u>this</u> history...and we will have a wonderful painting
in a place of honor.

Less than three months
later, on September 18,
1897, the foundations for
the main building were in
and the Rev. Dr. F. K.
Huntzinger, President of
the Board, laid the cornerstone. The building had a
front of 115´ and a depth
of 76´ facing the north.
The height to the top of
the dome was 105´.
The main building was
three stories high and the
wings two stories. The cost
of the farm, building and
furnishings totaled about
$40,000, of which $7,000
was for the 105-acre farm.

Cornerstone Laying
Program

Sept., 1899 - Orphans' Home Paper; Instructions, notes,
directions, & etc. Pertaining to the day of Dedication,
Sept. 14th.

Dinner will be furnished at the Home at 50 cents.
Supper at 35 Cents. Sandwiches and hot coffee are for

sale on the grounds. Confectioneries are also for sale. A limited number of horses can be accommodated in the farm barn. The rest will have to take care of their own horses. If they find it too much trouble to bring feed along, they can purchase feed from the hostler for the right figure. The profits of everything that is sold on any part of the ground or buildings go into the treasury of our Orphans' Home. Dedication in the presence of the Rev. Dr. Samuel Laird, Synod President.

Every one is expected to serve as a committee to bring the whole program to an orderly and successful end. Since our reservoir is not yet built, every one is requested not to waste any water at any of the spigots on the grounds or in the Building.

A card in every room will show the name and purpose of the room. There is a large tablet in the hall, on which is noted the portion of the building furnished or completed by various parties.

An early photograph of the original Topton Orphans' Home.

**Here are sketches of
the first and second floor.**

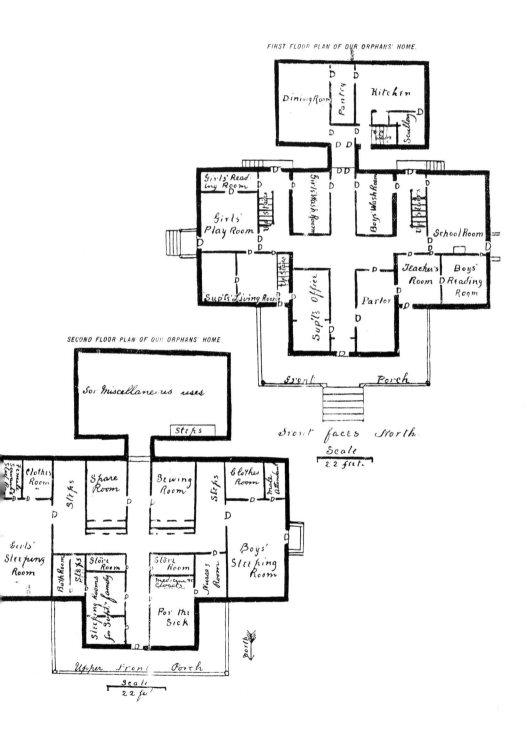

The Trustees now faced the staggering task of paying off this huge debt. One zealous Trustee, Walter Bieber, felt that an excursion to Gettysburg to tour the battlefield would be a

popular fund-raising project. On October 2, 1897, 360 persons boarded the first train leaving Allentown. Other sections were added until 10 special trains were included, with 5,000 persons aboard.

Walter Bieber

This was the beginning of the Annual Autumn Leaf Excursions to Gettysburg. We must recall that this was just over 30 years after the end of the Civil War, so it was recent and living history. These annual trips continued for 21 years, until they became a World War I casualty in 1917. $38,457 was realized through these famous excursions. At the start of the 100th Anniversary year, plans are being made to resurrect the Annual Autumn Leaf Excursions, to the delight of all.

A Committee of Visitors was appointed by the Ministerium of Pennsylvania to make an annual inspection of the Orphans' Home.

These were exciting days in America, fresh from a victory in its war with Spain. The last decade of the old century, soon to be known as the "gay nineties," was over and a young nation's great industrial expansion was beginning.

For Rev. Heilman, there was little time to join the cheering for Dewey and Hobson and Teddy Roosevelt. The family was growing almost daily. The supervision of the Home and farm, along with the task of raising funds to meet expenses and pay off the debt required a Herculean effort. Boys had moved into the main building. More orphans came. The school expanded. The farm work was done, *but farm work is never REALLY done, is it?*

Rev. Heilman is careful to include the details; he's accurate in all things. The following, a program from 1896 refers to "whole orphans" and "half orphans." Apparently, whole orphans (those without any parents) were given preference over "half orphans" (those with one parent.) It also announces the <u>Orphans' Home Paper</u>. This gives us a clear understanding of how important this small paper was, right from the start.

For many years we Lutherans have felt the need of ampler accommodations for our fatherless children, and particularly also have we felt the need of some institution where the motherless children, the homeless and the destitute may be clothed and fed, and enjoy the advantages of a Christian training.

A year or more ago, our heavenly Father, through the Holy Spirit, moved the Reading Conference to undertake the erection of a Home, such as circumstances plainly pointed out that we needed. Our Synod heartily endorsed the movement, and the work of putting up such a Home has at once begun.

A farm of about 105 acres, located a few squares south of the borough of Topton, was purchased for the sum of $7,000.00. This farm has on it good springs, lying about 60 feet higher than the building site. The location selected is in the very midst of the stronghold of Lutheranism in our Synod—midway between Reading and Allentown. The Home Buildings are now going up, and will be under roof in a few weeks. The Buildings should be ready for occupancy by next spring. The main Building is 117 feet long. An extra Building is annexed in the rear for Kitchen, Dining Room, etc. The cost of these Buildings, including the furnishing, the surroundings, etc., will be about $30,000.00

The doors of this Institution are not only to be open to the needy and destitute children of Berks County, in which the Buildings are located, but it is the object of the Board of Trustees to provide a Home for homeless children in our Synod—for whole orphans such as may knock at our doors, and for the half orphans and others for whom our Synod has theretofore had no provision whatever. Of course, every application will be carefully looked into, and only such will be admitted who are destitute of good homes, and to whom the church owes a home.

The farm purchased, and the buildings erected, will have to be paid by voluntary contributions from those in sympathy with this work. We are, at this time, confronted with many heavy bills which ought to be paid. We believe that many of our Lutheran friends, congregations, Sunday schools, societies, etc., beyond the bounds of our Conference would cheerfully contribute handsomely towards this noble work, if they had an invitation and opportunity to do so.

We hereby kindly ask for liberal contributions towards our Topton Orphans' Home. Every gift will be most thankfully received and promptly acknowledged in our Orphans' Home Paper.

The Orphans' Home Paper is published every month, price 50 cents per year. It keeps you constantly posted in all our work here, contains much practical information on our church, and is sent to any address.

The Superintendent moved into the farm house at Topton last spring; he has already orphans in his care; he is glad to have you come to visit the place and to see our work; and he is always ready, if his time allows, to present the orphans' cause to any congregation, society, etc. in our Synod.

We pray that you may give this circular your careful and prayerful consideration, and to encourage this our work at Topton with your prayer and gifts.

Sincerely Yours,

U. P. HEILMAN, Supt.

As we searched through the histories, we find blessed little of a personal nature about Rev. Heilman. *(Rev. Raker did give us insights into Mrs. Vesta Heilman; see Chapter 4.)* It was non-stop work, early 'til late. He and his wife had to super-vise the Home and farm, along with the constant task of raising funds. And, while they DID have the foresight to have a monthly publication, it certainly didn't have the reach needed to bring in <u>all</u> the funds needed. See how ANY example could be turned into a reason to give money.

> *May 1898, **Chewing gum** - Now, girls, do not be alarmed. We will not scold you this time. If you should once accidentally see yourselves in the looking glass, you would have grief enough. The reason we write now is to show you what a Sunday-school class of little girls did lately. They were chewing gum. (Maybe some of you have seen girls chewing gum and therefore know what we are talking about.)*
>
> *Well, their teacher asked them how much does tutti frutti cost them a week. Some said 2 cents, some 3, some 4. Now, said the teacher, would you not during this Lent season, be willing to do without gum and give those few pennies every Sunday here in the Orphans' Box to build a Home at Topton for poor orphans? They said they would. During last Lent, that class gathered over $4 for our Home, which is now in our treasury. Well, that was nice. Thanks to you, good teacher, for a wise suggestion; thanks to you, dear kind girls, for your self-denial.*

Suddenly, all of the tremendous progress stopped. We have only a brief account of his death from pneumonia on April 10, 1900 at the age of 50. Today, pneumonia isn't even a serious disease, merely a 'bother.' It can be cured in a week with about 28 tablets and $5 on your co-pay prescription card. WE have the medicine to cure it.

Rev. Heilman didn't. He was pushing himself day and night and didn't have enough strength to fight the swift, ravaging disease. From the July 1900 issue:

> *Rev. Heilman took a chill during a trip to Schuylkill Haven, where he had gone to preach for an ailing brother, on April 1. He returned to the Home on the following Monday, but kept planning and mentally working for the welfare of the institution until*

Thursday, when he was persuaded to take to his bed, his cold having developed into pleuro-pneumonia.

Loving hands and hearts of his friends of town ministered to his wants. On Saturday, his condition became worse. He was delirious during Sunday night and kept sinking till the end. He died on Tuesday afternoon at 4 p.m., April 10, 1900. He reached the age of 50 years, four months and five days. Thus passed a good man in the service of God and His church on earth.

The Heilman family:
(from left) Jennie,
Rev. Uriah P. Heilman, Carrie, Mrs.
Alvesta Heilman and William.

A burial plot was laid out near the main building and here on April 16th, his mortal remains were placed. Sermons were preached in English and German.

A monument to his memory was donated and erected by P.F. Eisenbrown, Sons & Co., Reading, Pa., and was dedicated on May 7, 1902.

RESOLUTIONS BY THE BOARD OF TRUSTEES

Inasmuch as it has pleased our heavenly Father to remove from among us our esteemed friend and co-worker, Rev. U. P. Heilman, we desire to place on record our high appreciation of his worth and services as a member of our Board and a Superintendent of our Orphans' Home.

Therefore be it:

Resolved, I That we bear our unanimous testimony to the faithfulness and diligence with which he discharged his official duties, the usefulness of his services and the success of his labors for the institution.

Resolved, II That we hereby express our high appreciation of his character as honest, truthful, sincere, upright and consistently Christian; of his earnest devotion to the interests

Heilman Monument

of the Home, for which he prayed and labored constantly and to the full extent of the measure of the faith and strength which were given him, and of his valuable services in the Board in which he proposed many useful measures and gave much good counsel.

Resolved, III That we express also our deep sorrow and sense of loss to ourselves and to the Home, and that we extend to his bereaved wife and children our sincere sympathy, with the prayer that the God of all consolation may comfort and sustain them.

23

*Resolved, IV That a copy of these resolutions be sent to
Mrs. Heilman, and that they be recorded in our
minutes.*

*M. C. Horine, J. J. Kuendig,
E. S. Wertz*

Rev. Heilman believed. He saw the Home where none
existed. He made the dream come real. He got it going in
the right direction and gave it everything he had.

Just before presstime, we received and will share some
anecdotes from Rev. Heilman's granddaughter, Mrs.
Harriet Heilman Stapleton of Palmetto, FL. She writes:

"I have a letter dated 1883 from Allentown, PA in which
Uriah P. Heilman asks a Rev. Renninger to come to
Ballietsville on Friday, July 20 at 8 p.m. to perform a marriage ceremony. He writes, 'I wish to enter into holy wed-
lock with Miss Vesta E. Moyer.' I think his first wife passed
away and there were no children.

"In 1894, he composed and published a small handbook
titled 'Teacher's Devotional Handbook' consisting of prayers
for many occasions. My family uses the table prayers. It
gives us a great sense of connection to him.

"Every morning that the main building was being built,
Rev. Heilman visited the construction site and prayed there.
It's believed that this is where he caught the pneumonia
which caused his death."

Chapter 3

1900– THE MOST PRECARIOUS YEAR!

T he year <u>started</u> splendidly. 1900 was hailed as the first year of the century, with as much excitement as we're already feeling about the year 2000. (Yes, we know that the century <u>really</u> started January 1, 1901, but almost everyone celebrated as 1900 came in!)

As The Lutheran Home got started in a strong manner, we're certain that the Trustees, ministers and congregations were jubilant. Things were going well. The main building was up, dedicated and occupied. It certainly was an impressive sight as you drove your horse and buggy up the hill from Topton. Orphans were being cared for. Rev. & Mrs. Heilman were working tirelessly, supervising the Home and farm, caring for the growing number of orphans, trying to raise funds to meet expenses.

His sudden death from pneumonia on April 10 was truly <u>devastating</u> news. The finances were NOT strong. Everything was just getting started. With the Superintendent struck down, the Board had to save the institution. In our opinion, the Orphans' Home was in its most perilous condition in 1900...without a leader, deeply in debt, new and struggling. In retrospect, it's likely that ANY adverse situation could have easily sunk this frail craft. As we'll see, the small team pulled together and, with Divine guidance, made it through these perilous times.

Rev. Heilman's hard-working widow, Vesta, became the temporary head while the Trustees searched for a successor. She was given high praise and thanks for stepping in during these most difficult circumstances. Mrs. Heilman showed "splendid executive ability" and was well loved by the orphans. This was one strong lady. Just a heartbeat before, it had been a dynamic couple. Abruptly, she was left by herself to manage without him. What an assignment!

From the Nov. 1900, issue:

> *It has been reported that Mrs. Heilman would remain at the Home as a teacher. She will remain at the home and teach but she will naturally be a great deal more than simply a teacher. There is no one who understands the management of the Home as she does, because she has been here from the very beginning.*
>
> *Mrs. Heilman has ingratiated herself in the hearts of the orphans, the community, the church at large , and the new superintendent and his wife are not jealous of it. There is certainly no work in which she could engage which would be more in accord with the work of her husband, who lies buried near the Home, than to continue her noble, self-sacrificing work of love at the Home.*

Years later, Rev. Raker, in May, 1907, the final issue he edited, we find this loving article under her photo:

MRS. VESTA E. HEILMAN

> *Mrs. Heilman needs no introduction to most of the friends of our Home. Her name and the name of her husband, the Rev. U. P. Heilman, will always be a synonym for the Orphans' Home at Topton. They laid the foundations of our Home deep and strong. They labored unceasingly in the morning twilight, before the breaking of day, when Orphans' Home work in Berks County was not as popular as it is today.*
>
> *In this great work they continued until Father Heilman fell by the wayside, and lies buried at the Orphans' Home. It was but natural for the Board of Trustees to look to Mrs. Heilman when a matron was needed at*

our Home. She has three children, Jennie, Carrie and Willie. The two daughters are teaching school, and the son will graduate at the Normal School, Kutztown, next Spring, and is preparing for Muhlenberg College, and for the Gospel ministry.

The death of Rev. Heilman raised MANY questions in a time without "instant communicatons." People had to WAIT days or weeks to find out what was going on. The Board had early recognized the widespread readership and educational value of the <u>Orphans' Home Paper</u>.

Now, they had really 'created a monster,' as it WAS widely read each month and the readers were worried that it would be dropped. With the outpouring of emotion following Rev. Heilman's death, they apparently received substantial mail about the continuation of the Home AND of the publication.

In today's jargon, we call the following article "damage control." Please note that, with the deadline for the May issue, it had to be put together in the second or third week of April. They did a splendid job of getting the stunning news out quickly.

From the May, 1900 issue:

THIS PAPER WILL BE CONTINUED

On the fourth page of every copy of the "Orphans' Home Paper", you will observe the words: "Published by the Board of Trustees." And while Rev. Heilman was the originator of the paper, and its sole and efficient editor, yet it was by action of the Board that it was established and continued. It will, by God's help, be so continued.

And though no one is able to take up the pen so suddenly laid down, yet it is the purpose that this little publication shall continue to be the advocate of the Home, to present its growth, conditions and wants to the people, and to be "devoted in particular to the interests of the Evangelical Lutheran Orphans' Home at Topton, Berks Co., Pa." Until a successor to our devoted Superintendent is elected and installed, the

*following committee will have charge of its
publication: Rev. A. M. Weber, Rev. S. L. Harkey, D.D.,
and Rev. M. C. Horine, D.D.*

Through May and June of
1900, the Board worked on the
monumental task of the prompt
replacement of Rev. Heilman.

Within two months, they found
a candidate, approved him
unanimously and...*then
something went wrong.*
This brief paragraph in the July
1900 issue speaks to the point
quite eloquently:

*REV. BERND
DOES NOT ACCEPT*

Rev. F. K. Bernd

*Rev. F. K. Bernd, who was unanimously elected to the
superintendency of our Orphans' Home, has felt
inclined to decline the call extended to him. He
appreciates the honor the Board of Trustees has thus
conferred upon him and heartily thanks them for it.*

*He took the matter under careful and earnest
consideration and was not able to decide for a long
time. But after much thought, he came to the
conclusion that he was not fitted for the place. It is,
therefore, with feelings of regret that he felt himself
constrained to decline the call. He trusts that we may
soon be able to find a suitable man.*

In spite of all the turmoil in trying to replace Rev.
Heilman, life went on. On August 16, the first Donation
Day (later Anniversary Day) was held, with excellent attendance. Each succeeding year, the celebration was held on
the third Thursday of August.

The Anniversary Day celebration has attracted uncounted
thousands of people to Topton to attend the program and
tour the buildings.

That tradition has continued for almost a hundred years. New generations come to experience Anniversary Day and enjoy the entertainment and the delicious foods. They also learned about the growing mission.

> *July 1900 - August 16, 1900: Annual Donation Day, All charitable institutions have what is known as an annual donation day, when its friends flock to it by the hundreds and even thousands to see the place, to hear addresses on the work, to have a day of recreation and the meeting of friends, and last, but not least, to bring something good (good cheer, good goods, good money), to the home. The third Thursday in August has been set apart by the Board of Trustees as such a day for our Topton Orphans' Home. Arrangements are to be made with the railroad company to carry you there and home again at greatly reduced rates. Prominent speakers will be there to address you. The children with their bright faces and contented hearts will be there to greet you.*
>
> *Preparations will be made to properly satisfy your hunger, or you can bring what you will for this purpose. We want to see every one of you there and all your friends whom you can bring. Commence now to arrange your work so that you will not miss all this. Above all, do not forget the day.*

The search for a new superintendent continued through the summer of 1900. Apparently, the geographic area of the search was widened. Mrs. Heilman was taking care of the entire operation with great skill. Then, just in time for the October issue, we read an enthusiastic article, full of joy, praise and (probably) relief.

OUR NEW SUPERINTENDENT

> *Just in time to introduce him! Rev. J. H. Raker, of Lebanon, has been elected superintendent of this Home. He comes well equipped, mentally and physically, for the work. Best of all his heart is in it. He and his wife take charge on October 2d. Mrs. Heilman, we are glad*

29

to say, remains also, as teacher of the little orphans. We hand the editorship of this paper over to him, with one request, that he permit us to introduce him more fully to you, our kind readers, by a picture and a biography in the next issue. God bless and strengthen our new superintendent and his wife.

And so, at the REAL start of the new century, Rev. Raker took the reins. I'm sure that, with a great deal of relief, the Board members wished each other a 'Happy New Year and a Happy 20th Century!"

Chapter 4

BACK ON TRACK

The Rev. John H. Raker, D.D.
1901-1907

An excellent insight into Rev. John Raker's character is contained in the introduction by author Dick Cowen to <u>Papa Raker's Dream</u>, his history of the Good Shepherd Home (1908-1988):

> I've taken my approach for this book on The Good Shepherd Home from a lesson Dr. John Raker, its co-founder, learned in 1900.
>
> He had just received a call to be superintendent of the struggling new Lutheran Orphans' Home at Topton, Pennsylvania. The Topton Home had twenty-four children, a new building and a large debt. The support for charity was not as easy as in later years.
>
> He asked a number of persons how to go about the work of meeting the debt and expenses of that home. He personally canvassed most congregations of the Reading Conference.
>
> And the answer he got was that he should prepare one great sermon and preach that all over.

The Rev. John H. Raker, D.D.

He went so far as selecting the text, Matthew 18:5. "And whoso shall receive one such little child in my name receiveth me."

But among other persons, he asked Dr. William A. Passavant of Pittsburgh, the great inner mission champion. Passavant responded, "Little incidents directly from the home will do more good than any sermon you or I, or anybody else, will preach."

After that, John Raker asked a farmer near Topton who replied, "We have our ministers to preach big sermons. When you come around, we want to hear something about the Home."

That settled the big sermon question. That sermon was never preached. But the message he spread about life at the Topton Home brought gifts that removed its entire debt in his first year and raised $5,000 for an Old People's Building before he left.

Dick Cowen*
May 1988

The Rev. John H. Raker, D.D., a man of boundless energy and indomitable faith, **was** prepared to dedicate his life to the task of caring for children and old people. We who know of the splendid success of The Good Shepherd Home in Allentown, PA aren't terribly surprised when we read the details about the man who started it all. He didn't start there. He began this work at Topton.

When Rev. Raker came, the Orphans' Home was heavily in debt. It was a new institution and needed EVERYTHING. By 1900, the debt greeting Rev. Raker was about $50,000, a huge amount in those days. He rolled up his sleeves and started at once to raise money. *In one 18-day period, he raised $11,000! What a remarkable ability!*

In less than four years, the Home was debt-free, even though a reservoir had been constructed in 1902 to supply

---

* Permission to use granted by author Dick Cowen.

the buildings with running water.

Before Rev. Raker left the Home in 1907, he had accumulated a fund of $5,000 for a proposed Old Folks' Home.

Rev. Raker was a seasoned and effective minister. He was well-traveled, spoke English and German, and had traveled west to Indian Territory, north

Reservoir - Gift of Charles Breneiser, Sr.

through New England and Nova Scotia, through our southern states, and east to seven countries in Europe. He was an accomplished, eloquent speaker, a top-notch fundraiser... and all of this before his 40th birthday. If you haven't met Rev. Raker before, prepare to be impressed with his biography from the Nov. 1900 issue:

Rev. John Henry Raker, son of Conrad Hoffman Raker and Susan (Dornsife) Raker, was born at Raker, Northumberland Co., Pa. on Jan. 1, 1863. He attended the public schools at Raker and Nanticoke, Pa., and a select school at Northumberland, Pa.

After teaching for two years, he prepared for college in the Academic Department of Muhlenberg College in 1884. He entered the Freshman class in 1885 and was graduated in 1889.

He was the superintendent of Emmanuels Ev. Lutheran Sunday-school at Raker, Pa. for three years; St. Mark's Sunday-school in south Allentown for three years and the Springfield Sunday-school at Mt. Airy, Philadelphia, for two years. During his senior year in college, he was instrumental in organizing St. Stephen's Lutheran Sunday-school in west Allentown.

The school was opened on Mar. 12, 1889 in the Seventh Ward Public School House, and has resulted in the organization of a congregation having 66 members and a Sunday-school numbering 165. Of it Dr. Wackernagel, the pastor, says: "the chief agitator in the enterprise was J.H. Raker '89."

During his senior vacation, he was one of the State speakers for the Constitutional Amendment, and averaged three speeches per day for over four weeks, speaking one to one and a half hours at a time. Immediately after graduation, he went to Southern Kansas and Indian Territory, where he assisted Rev. E. E. Schantz in his mission work.

He entered the Theological Seminary at Mt. Airy in 1889 and graduated in 1892. He also studied in the National School of Elocution and Oratory (now the Neff College of Oratory), from which he was graduated on May 27, 1892. Two days later he was ordained to the office of the Holy Ministry of the Evangelical Lutheran Church at Reading, Pa.

During his Senior vacation at the Seminary, he had charge of St. John's Mission at Pen Argyl, Pa. He received a unanimous call from this mission and entered upon his pastorate after ordination. He was its pastor for six years. The first year, 70 members were admitted. In three years, it became self-supporting and the first year the $1,000 church debt was paid within $50.

In the Spring of 1898, he accepted a unanimous call from Holy Trinity Evangelical Lutheran Church of Lebanon, Pa. During the first year's pastorate, 54 members were received into the church. In less than two years, the church's debt was reduced over $1,600.00.

Rev. Raker has considerable experience on the lecture platform, for which his natural talents, extensive travels, keen observation and close study have well fitted him. During his college course, he gave many stereopticon lectures and thus made many friends in the churches of Lehigh, Bucks and Northampton Counties, which will be a great help to him in his work for the Home.

In 1894, under leave of absence from the vestry of his church and the mission committee, he visited Europe. From June to October, he traveled in England, Ireland, France, Belgium, Holland, Germany, Switzerland and Italy. On this trip, he gathered material for his illustrated lectures.

In 1895, he made a three months' trip through the New England states, New Brunswick and Nova Scotia, producing a lecture on "Nova Scotia." In 1896, he traveled through the southern states, speaking on: "Bible Lecture", "Our Old Home, or Observation and Experience in Europe", "Get the Focus", "Wooing the Maiden, or An Alpine Experience", "How to Help and Be Helped." Here is a choice for the church societies to raise considerable sums of money for the Orphans' Home.

Rev. Raker married Miss D. Estella Weiser of Lebanon, Pa., on June 5th, 1899 in Holy Trinity Church, Lebanon. She is a descendant of Conrad Weiser, the great Indian interpreter and statesman of the early history of Pennsylvania. She is a graduate of the Myerstown High School and was a student at the Neff College of Oratory in Philadelphia. She has been teaching elocution for over four years and will teach elocution, music and physical culture at the Home."

To understand the success of Rev. John H. Raker's work throughout his life, we must understand that he was truly a SUPERB communicator. In his time, before e-mail, the Internet, fax machines, movies and TV...there was the spoken word. However, it's typical of Rev. Raker to be 'first with the best communications.' In January of 1903, the

Kutztown Telephone Exchange opened the area for telephone service. It was thought of as more of a frill than a utility. However, the Lutheran Orphans' Home was **one of the first seven parties** to receive telephone service in the Topton area!

People went to hear lectures. They read books. Ministers gave rousing sermons! (They would have snorted at our present-day insistence on giving God but one puny hour on Sunday!) Here's a splendid article from the Jan. '02 issue.

If you want to get the flavor of it, get up, walk around, wave your arms, read it out loud with great feeling! <u>It sings!</u>

THE CHURCH YEAR

This is an age that likes novelty, that is always looking for something new to attract and amuse—an age of progress that is leaving old things behind. It may seem strange to hold up before such an age an old Prayer book—many centuries old—and choose it in preference to all things that are new, and join a church because it clings to things that are old.

It may seem strange to prize its teachings of a Christian year, whose chief characteristic is that it treads old paths, and year by year gives the same prayers, the same collects, epistles and gospels, the same Scripture lessons, the same feasts and fasts—doing this year as we did last year and the year before, as even our fathers did in their time of old. Yet is is a fact, and I am proud to acknowledge it.

We must remember that life is made up of things new and old. The newer some things are, the better we like them; the older other things are, the more we prize them. Life demands both.

There is a constant variety; change, even novelty, there must be, for some things are worn out by constant use. We get tired of them. There are, also, those things which age renders more precious; which constant use endears to us.

This is illustrated in our social life. Upon the surface are the novelties, the recreations, the entertainments, the gaieties, the merry laugh.

Beneath the surface is home life, where loves of long duration cement the times that bind hearts together, where the old associations, the familiar pictures, the furnishings; yea, the dear old walls of our childhood's home, make it all seem so precious to us. We tire of recreations. We never tire of home.

Upon the surface of the ocean are the light airy vessels, good only for pleasure, skipping about upon the waves, pleasing us with their antics. Upon the same waters are the large, well-ballasted vessels, ploughing steadily, unchangeable, towards a desired haven. They represent the gaiety and the seriousness of life—its pleasures and its business.

So it is in regard to the Christian year. There is variety in its changing seasons, in which Christian truth and worship are represented to us, now in festival, again in fast. The Christmas carol thrills us with joy; the Lenten hymn carries its sad appeal to tender hearts. But, taken all in all, underneath the variety, there is a thought that represents that permanence and stability which every soul needs.

Who would care for a changeable God, or a changeable Gospel, or a changeable faith; and can we be content to invent a changeable worship to represent what must ever wield the same influence upon the human soul?

To me, the Christian year may be likened to God's mercies—new every morning, yet always the same. So the round of services, under the guidance of a Christian year, are new, though always old; new in their refreshment, but always old in fact. There is something permanent in our religion, something we can learn to love, as we love the hymns we learned in childhood's day.

There is the old, old church to work for and to pray for and to live for; sweet communions and solemn vows as old as the centuries, that we can prize. Such a church is a home.

And not least among its blessing is the fact that the Christian year allows no one-sided ideas of truth. We are not subject to the caprice of any individual minister who is apt to magnify one phase of truth at the expense of others equally important.

Nor does it permit error in doctrine, as its teaching keeps before us, in the course of the year, the many-sidedness of truth, and we have it presented to us in all its phases, while pastor and people tread together well-tried paths of devotion, and travel over well-known avenues of thought, and journey together as they visit the places where Christ wrought his mighty deeds and spake His blessed words, and learn together the blessed truths of the Gospel.

I thank God that my lot is cast in the church that sets her face against the idea of novelty in worship to entertain the people, and magnifies the idea of permanence in a worship that must lead each soul into the presence of Jehovah.

There is in the Christian year another thought. It is the same, and yet it is different each year. There is stability on the Divine side, but progress on the human side. Like all great sciences, we know only the elements. Our study and use denote our progress in that science. So in our religious life. Can anyone intelligently repeat the Lord's Prayer every day in the year and have it express no new thought?

Can we read the Bible every day and know nothing more than we did last year?

Can Christ be presented as the central thought in every service and in every season, and we know no more of His person and His love than we did the year before?

Can a whole Christian year laden with truth pass, and we be as ignorant as we were before the year began?

While we want the year of grace to be the same, it is for us to make it different in its influence upon our lives. We may use it with holier minds, truer penitence, livelier faith, warmer love, steadier resolution, and its prayers burning with a brighter flame upon the altar of our hearts. Thus the church remains the same, while we are progressive. Such is the purpose of a "Christian year."

—*The Rev. John H. Raker*

**The Raker family, circa 1904:
from left: Mrs. Estella Raker, daughters Ruth
(top) and Roberta, Rev. John H. Raker**

This man was a 'ball of fire.' More and more orphans came. By 1905, they were up to 68 orphans. Support was solid and strong. His wife, Estella, was the matron, much loved by the children **and** a very effective partner. You can get a feeling of the amount of <u>her</u> work by checking out <u>his</u> Sunday traveling schedule! (What's not included is how the matron spent HER Sundays!)

Sept. 1901

HOW THE SUPERINTENDENT SPENDS HIS SUNDAYS

On Saturday, August 18, we left Topton at 1 o'clock p.m. for Harrisburg. Took the trolley from Harrisburg for Progress. Here we were met by a member, who took us to his home for supper and afterwards to church. At 7:30 we preached at Wenrich's Church, Rev. P. A. Behler, pastor. From here, the pastor took us to his home at Grantville. On Sunday morning, we were taken to the Shellsville Church and addressed the Sunday-school before church, preached a harvest home sermon, and after some announcements by the pastor, we preached an Orphans' Home sermon.

From here we were taken to Palmyra, where we preached in the evening. In the morning we arose before five o'clock, walked one mile to the station and reached Topton on Monday morning after 7 o'clock. This is how we spend our Sundays. Rev. Behler has selected the Sunday nearest Reformation Day when all his congregations will take an offering of money and provisions for our Home. After all our congregations have selected one day of the year in which offerings will be taken for our Home, there will be no need of the Superintendent to be out every Sunday.

Rev. Raker had a way with words on almost ANY subject, but listen to him speak about the baptism of his first child. We get a peek at his droll sense of humor, which was to serve him very well throughout his entire career!

Sept. 1901

RUTH DOROTHEA RAKER

Many people complained that they did not have an opportunity to see Ruth on Donation Day, and on that account we give her picture. She was born on the 24th of December, 1900; baptized on January 11, 1901 by the Rev. A. C. Schenk and the Rev. W. U. Kistler assisting.

The baptism was performed in the superintendent's office in the presence of all the orphans, who joined in the baptismal service and sang especially prepared hymns. The water used was from Luther's well in Wittenberg, Germany.

She is the first child born in the Lutheran Orphans' Home at Topton, Pa. She was born in the evening of the nineteenth century and baptized in the morning of the twentieth century. Ruth has never been sick for one minute, as far as we know, and has laughed oftener than cried.

All that saw her said that she was such a beautiful child, and then concluded by saying that she looked just like her father. How to reconcile these two expressions may be difficult, but remember we are simply quoting.

Ruth Dorothea Raker

The enlarged swimming dam apparently needed a name, which generated a contest. The winning entry (six votes) was "THE ESTELLA," named for Mrs. Raker. ("Lake Raker" only garnered one vote.)

THE ESTELLA

There is about one inch of ice on our lake.

We have about two tons of ice in our ice house yet, and have been supplying Topton with ice for over one month.

Last winter, the Topton people said when July comes, there would be no ice at the Orphans' Home. We had *all the ice we needed and are now selling it at $2.00 per ton from the ice house.*

It is truly a blessing to have Rev. Raker's eloquent articles on a variety of subjects. They bring the past alive as almost nothing else can. For example, let's go back and see what the Lord's Day was like at the Topton Orphans' Home almost a century ago.

Sept. 1901

SUNDAY AT THE HOME

As we have no visitors at the Home on Sundays, it may be of interest to our readers to know how the Sunday is spent at the Home. In order to spend the Sunday properly, we must always get ready on Saturday.

On Saturday evening, the children are all washed and their clothes are gotten ready for Sunday. At 7 o'clock Sunday morning the rising bell is rung. Breakfast at 7:30. After the necessary work at the Home is finished, they all get ready for Sunday-school at 10 o'clock, which is in session for one hour. Dinner at 11:30; Heilman's catechism from 2 to 3 o'clock; supper at 5 o'clock, worship at 7 o'clock, after which the smaller children retire. Luther League with the larger children, using the Luther League topics, after which all retire.

We have mentioned the Sunday's worship and work, but some may ask what do the children do the rest of the time. Some read, or gather berries, apples, pears, etc., to eat. Our children are perfectly free on Sunday. Of course there is a marked distinction between Sunday and any other day of the week.

It's widely known that Rev. Raker and the Board of Trustees differed on the mission of the Home. Rev. Raker's inner voice took him in a different direction. So we see how Divine guidance charts different pathways for us all. And they are ALL in Divine order.

If one studies Rev. Raker's writings and follows his life, it's very clear that, while The Orphans' Home was CLOSE to his 'call,' it was not <u>exactly</u> his right place. He had a vision, made it come real and established a world-class institution, The Good Shepherd Home in Allentown, PA.

He began his seven-year effort at the Topton Orphans' Home on the first day of the new century, took strong charge of a deeply wounded institution and left it in splendid shape for his own life work.

Feb. 1907

RESIGNED AND ACCEPTED A CALL

The Rev. J. H. Raker, Superintendent of the Lutheran Orphans' Home at Topton, has resigned as Superintendent and accepted a call from Grace Lutheran Church, Allentown. He expects to enter upon his new duties on or before the first of May next.

In the May 1907 issue, Rev. Raker bids a "SECOND FAREWELL," noting that he was asked to edit and mail the May issue and notes,

"We had not expected to do this, especially as we were exceedingly busy getting ready to move, but we always try to be as good as our word, and promised to edit the paper and return from Allentown to Topton and spend two days and mail the paper."

In your imagination, picture Rev. Raker walking through the Home late on the last evening, trying not to make any noise as he checked the sleeping children and the empty rooms which had rung with the laughter of his own family. This article, also from the May 1907 issue, is most poignant and elegant.

THE LAST NIGHT AT THE ORPHANS' HOME

Did you ever take note of the fact, that the things for which you long the most ardently, are often the things from which you shrink and hesitate, when the time of their fulfillment approaches? So it is with respect to leaving the Orphans' Home. The day is over, the work is not all done, but the foreign matter in the crying child's eye has been removed, all have retired and everything is quiet. The children's last good night is repeating itself like the waves on the quiet lake caused by a falling pebble.

We think of the past and try to look into the untried future. The furniture has been sent away, the rooms look large and bare, but we must say good-night. Let us meet again in earth and in heaven.

One year later, Rev. Raker founded The Good Shepherd Home for Crippled Children and Old People in Allentown, PA. His years of achievement at the Home gave a firm foundation to Rev. Henry, who followed him.

As we celebrate our first century, Good Shepherd and The Lutheran Home at Topton, two strong Lutheran institutions, are currently working together on a number of cooperative projects. The Lord moves in mysterious ways.

Chapter 5

A Brief Mystery

The Rev. Friedrich Holter
1908

Naturally, the search had begun for another Superintendent, following Rev. Raker's departure. The Board of Trustees knew full well the necessity of having strong leadership at the Orphans' Home. Therefore, in the May, 1907 issue, we note the following article, clarifying that, while they were searching for a new Superintendent, Rev. J. O. Henry would take over temporarily. Note the very positive comments and solid support.

The Rev. J. O. Henry, of Topton, Pa., has been appointed temporary Superintendent of our Orphans' Home at Topton. Brother Henry is the proper person to take charge of the Home, on account of his location, inclination and marriage.

As Rev. Henry lives near the Orphans' Home, it makes it possible for him to continue his parish work and still devote some time to the management of the Home. His friendly inclination for children will greatly help him, for native kindness will accomplish more among children than great experience without kindness. The last and not the least, he is the son-in-law of the great Orphans' Home man in the Allentown Conference.

We have reference to Mr. Sefing, who is able and always willing to assist in the management of the Home. We have not been requested to say it, but

Brother Henry, among many others, would make a good permanent Superintendent of the Home. With these few words we introduce the temporary Superintendent of our Home.

This is very informative. It seems that Rev. Henry had 'a friend in court.' It was his father-in-law, a strong supporter. Additionally, it certainly **didn't** hurt him to be in the right place at the right time.

He was praised for his friendly inclination for children. So, he got a 'tryout' without having to leave his present parish. He was the "lead article" in the June 1907 issue:

THE REV. J. O. HENRY

As is well known by all who take an interest in our Orphans' Home at Topton, the position of Superintendent, made vacant through the resignation of the Rev. J. H. Raker, who left the Home on April 23, is filled temporarily by the Rev. J. O. Henry, Pastor of Topton Parish. We had hoped to have Rev. Henry's photograph grace the first page of this number, but when the pastor was approached on this point, his modesty was so great that he gave a decided negative to this request, and yet, if we can manage to obtain his cut*, you will find it at the head of this article.

The formal, stylized writing of an older age is refreshing in these days of bad grammar and 'sound bites.'

---

* Author's note: (Using his 'cut' had nothing to do with bleeding. This was the term for a metal engraving. In the old days, a photographic negative was placed on a pre-coated zinc plate and exposed to light. Hydrochloric acid was used to 'cut' the lighter parts of the image away, thus the term: "cut.")

Take a closer look at the photo. You'll see the curved edges at the top. Translation: while Rev. Henry steadfastly refused to have a new photo taken, his wife provided a personal photo in an oval frame.

The same issue assures the reader that things are running well at the Home. Apparently, this was of great importance to reassure the readers, as it got ample space in a very small publication.

"Mrs. Vesta Heilman, widow of the late Rev. U. P. Heilman, is in the building and acting in the capacity of Matron. This is a temporary arrangement, to last at least until a permanent Superintendent is elected, and on the grounds.

Mrs. Heilman, it need not be told, knows how to manage. The Board was exceedingly fortunate to get her at this period."

As we journey through the first century of The Lutheran Home at Topton, we're fascinated at the character of the leaders. With only five in a century, we see that each had time to put his signature on an era.

But wait...there's one more. Rev. Friedrich Holter. In all the previous histories, he receives only a few sentences, leaving us with several questions. Why was he picked? Why didn't he stay? What's the real story? Everyone loves a mystery and we believe we can shed some light on this one.

Come and meet Rev. Holter through these highlights of his biography in the December, 1907 issue.

Read of his stunning successes in the "wild west" of South Dakota, Pennsylvania's Coal Region, where he learned and preached in Polish, challenges and accomplishments in New Jersey, plus his fund-raising efforts to establish an orphans' home in East India.

REV. FRIEDRICH HOLTER

Born in the village of Tweswoos, District of Doemitz, Mecklenberg-Schwerin, Germany, on April 29, 1858. He attended the parochial school of his native village under the instructorship of F. Wahler, who had charge for 52 years. In 1872, Rev. Friedrich Holter was confirmed by Pastor Rev. W. Wuestney.

The Rev. Friedrich Holter

After confirmation he was sent to the schools at Doemitz and Luebtheen, Mecklenberg-Schweirin, preparing for missionary work. He started for America and reached Hoboken on the 12th of September, 1880. Then to Illinois, to the Wartburg Seminary, of the German Jawa-Synade, to study theology.

After seminary, he was sent to do mission work among the German Lutheran settlers in Plainview, Douglas County, South Dakota. The Dakotas at that time were only territories and very sparsely settled. He was ordained by the Rev. G. A. Bischoff on April 15, 1883, at Plainview. A congregation was soon organized.

Rev. Holter took up a claim of 160 acres of government land. On a ten-acre plot, a small chapel (14′ x 22′) was erected. Other congregations were organized at Blumenthal, Plankington, Kimball and Belmont; preaching points were started at Mitchel and Mt. Vernon.

After two years of the most difficult kind of labor, he was sent to Sheldon, Ransom County, North Dakota. Work at two small disbanded congregations was begun anew and the congregations were soon re-established. Congregations were organized at Sheldon, Watson,

Casselton, Griswold, New Rockford, Coopertown,
Davenport and a branch at Fargo.

The early settlers lacked funds. Consequently, services
were conducted in public schools, private homes, and
on mission festivals in the open air. A small parsonage
was purchased at Sheldon and from this location he
visited the various congregations for six years. During
his stay in the Dakotas, on the commission of the
presidents of the Synod, he ordained four candidates,
one in South Dakota and three in North Dakota, and
placed them in fields which he had prepared.

He had to undergo many hardships. When his health
began to fail, he resigned his charge and resolved to go East
to restore his health. After a three-months' stay with his
uncle at Mauch Chunk, Pa., he accepted a call to Christ
Lutheran Church, Scranton, Pa., and on March 22, 1891, he
began work in his new field of labor. Through his guiding
influence, the disbanded congregation was again admitted
as a member of the Ministerium of Pennsylvania.

The chapel was in very poor condition, but through his
untiring and energetic efforts, the entire building was
remodeled, a tower erected, pews, altar, pulpit, stained
windows, baptismal font, pipe organ and bell and
smaller miscellaneous articles were purchased at great
expense. A parochial school was organized under his
instruction, and after several months a teacher was
procured. The congregation increased in membership,
as well as financially.

His interest was not confined to his own congregation
but to other churches as well—especially in Petersburg
and Providence, two suburbs of Scranton.

In Petersburg, St. Peter's Lutheran Church, which had
separated many years ago, was brought back to the
Ministerium of Pennsylvania. In Providence, where
many Polish Lutherans were living and working in the
coal mines, a new church was started. Rev. F. Holter

grew interested in these Pols and studied the language somewhat, then preached the gospel to them in their own native tongue.

He soon organized the "Emmanuel German-Polish Evan. Lutheran Church", bought and paid for two lots, and afterwards a fine church was erected. The congregation owns good property but belongs to the Missouri Synod. He also conducted service at Carbondale, Pa., and paved the way for the Evangelical Lutheran St. Paul's Church at that place.

By the death of Rev. A. Stuckert, St. Paul's Evangelical Lutheran Church, Jersey City, became vacant. He accepted their call and was installed as its pastor on Oct. 25, 1896. The congregation had been on the decline, but through the ever-ready, untiring and zealous efforts of Rev. F. Holter, prospered as never before. In 1898 a parsonage valued at about $3,800 was built, some thousand dollars of debts were paid and many repairs were made.

In 1905, the congregation was forced to sell its property to the Erie Railroad Co., which corporation proposed to open a cut through the heights of Jersey City. A new site valued at $10,000 was bought and a beautiful edifice valued at $56,000 was erected. This church was dedicated May 26, 1907. It is declared to be one of the most beautiful of the Lutheran churches.

Beside his pastorate, Rev. F. Holter holds the following offices: Since Dec. 1, 1899, chaplain at Snake Hill, where the penitentiary, the insane asylum and the home for the poor of Hudson County are situated; since 1900 he has been a member of the German Home Mission Board of the General Council, and was its recording secretary since that time.

Through his efforts, an orphans' home was established four years ago. He has been its treasurer since organization. Two years ago, he was appointed

*representative of the Gossner Mission in Berlin,
Germany, to collect money for mission purposes among
the Kols in East India. He sent more than five thousand
Marks to Berlin during this time.*

*On August 27, 1885, he was married to Miss Emma
Trapp at Sheldon, North Dakota. Her birthplace is
Stalp, Pammerania, Germany. They were blessed with
eleven children, seven of whom are living.*

The turning of the seasons continued, no matter who was
at the helm. And, as Rev. Heilman had left an ambitious
schedule, Rev. Holter stepped right in and kept it going.
More orphans came, were cared for, taught and helped.
The crops were planted, cultivated, harvested. Anniversary
Day was held. Things seemed to be under control.

We've mentioned above that Rev. Holter was an accomplished and well-traveled man. He spoke and wrote well.
He was persuasive, a hard worker, a fine fund-raiser and
had previously shown his heartfelt interest in the plight of
orphans long before taking this job. His compelling résumé
and personality got him the postition. His qualifications
were solid. **Well, then...what big things could push this
man to resign such a position so quickly?**

We submit that it probably wasn't the big things, but the
"little stuff" that probably did him in. Don't forget that we
were barely into this century, when most communication was
very personal. Very "one-to-one." Negative personal communication (gossip) gets his attention in the August, 1908
issue. Catch the tone here. It sets the scene for what follows.

*We feel obliged to make mention of a matter which,
perhaps, more than anything else, has been a great
detriment to our Home. We refer to gossip. We do this
in order that all may know our position in this regard.
From time to time, reports have been circulated about
the Home and happenings here which have had no
foundation whatever. And yet many have believed
such simply because some one told them, never for one
moment reflecting as to their validity. We dislike the*

*practice, and will not stand for it; and we ask the
assistance of all our well-wishers to root out this evil
practice as much as possible. If any rumors strike your
ears, test them and find out if there is any truth in
them. Visit the Home and see. Let us have a heart to
heart talk with each other. Nothing would delight us
more, and it would benefit us both.*

Too many years have passed to know exactly WHAT the
gossip was about. From later remarks, it would seem that
some people were voicing the general complaint that 'not
enough was being done.' (Tough to defend against.)

However, while gossip may be a quintessential part of
politics, we'll see that Rev. Holter apparently would have
none of it as regarded the Orphans' Home. Apparently, he
made his decision in November. Thus, in the December
1908 issue, he announces his resignation in a very
conciliatory and friendly message.

December 1908

*It may be a surprise to our readers that we are going
to leave this place again after such a short stay of only
one year. When we came on New Year's Day, 1908, we
came with the intention of remaining here, but are
sorry to say that it is impossible for us to do so under
the present circumstances; therefore, after a very
careful consideration, we came to the conclusion,
for various important reasons, to resign, which
resignation was handed in Nov. 20 and will go into
effect Jan. 1, 1909. It was accepted by the Board at the
meeting Dec. 1.*

*As we have received a unanimous call from St. Mark's
Lutheran congregation of Brooklyn, N.Y. and accepted
same, we will resume our regular ministerial work
there on this day. We kindly ask our dear readers
herewith to send all communications from this day to
the "Lutheran Orphans' Home, Topton, Pa.," as
somebody will be there to take care of the matter. We
hope that the Board will be able to find a suitable man*

for this place by that time.

As we are editing the January number of this paper, we will say a "Farewell word" to our friends in that issue. May God's richest blessing rest upon the Home in the future.

Well, Rev. Holter <u>was</u> polite, kind and conciliatory in December...but he "let it all hang out" in the January, 1909 issue. He really felt let down, and the reader gets the message loud and clear. At first, we were going to edit the long article, but it's only fair for you to read his reasoned and eloquent words. Please note especially his "reasons for our leaving." He shows concern for his wife's overwork and "gossips and slandering of some papers." My guess is that he meant local newspapers.

It's important to remember that this is a tough man. He survived rough years in North and South Dakota... starting up congregations under terrible circumstances. This is not a weakling. Using one of today's buzzwords, we'd say he became "stressed out" in this assignment. (It's fascinating to consider that, today The Lutheran Home has fine programs to help ministers with this kind of problem.)

But Rev. Holter's story is <u>not</u> of today. Full of frustration and sadness, Rev. Holter says goodbye in the January, 1909 issue. Note that history confirms that all of his suggestions <u>were</u> taken and implemented.

We promised in the last issue to say a "Farewell Word" in the January number, and this we shall do now.

Every institution of this kind needs a leader, who is the soul of the entire concern and is responsible for all the doings connected thereto; he must have full charge of everything. Such a leader is generally called Director or Superintendent. The duties of such a Director or Superintendent are laid down in the constitution and by-laws of such an institution.

The report of the Bethany Orphans' Home at Womelsdorf, Pa., 1908, says about the duties of the Superintendent: "Directing the heads of various departments; maintaining discipline in the spirit of the gospel; guarding against all waste; seeing to the supply of everything needed by the children; securing for them such comforts as the liberality of the church warrants; protecting them in their rights; leading them to appreciate their privileges; encouraging them to take advantage of their opportunities; holding out before them lofty ideals and cultivating in them the spirit of gratitude to God and His church for all the blessings which they enjoy in the Home, and to purchase the supplies and to do the corresponding business."

Truly, if a Superintendent tries to fulfill all these duties he has no time to waste, but must be active right along. To be the leader of such institution, it takes much wisdom and prayer.

Besides the Superintendent, and his wife as matron, a number of employees are necessary if the work which is connected thereto is to be done properly. We, at our institution, have at the present time eighty-five children, and, in accord with our judgment, the following employees are needed:

Three teachers, two for the main department and one for the kindergarten; one overseer of the boys, one overseer over the girls, an assistant matron, a janitor, a cook and a seamstress. All of these employees would be kept busy from morning to night, if the work is to be done as it should be. Our children are able to help, but they need a leader who shows them this work and how to do it properly. These children have been sent here to be educated in every way, and to do this the necessary assistance must be had. Without such helpers the work remains undone, and the Superintendent afterwards gets the blame for it.

The church should furnish the means which are needed. If this is not done, the whole cause has to suffer. It was well said by one of the members at our last meeting that we never had help enough. This is true. Therefore, we hope and pray that the coming Superintendent, whoever he may be, will get help enough to be able to do his work with joy and not in sorrow.

Since it has become known that we are going to leave and take up pastoral work again in Brooklyn, N.Y., we have received many letters in which the writers regret our going very much. We, therefore, feel it our duty to give reasons for our leaving.

First—To give our family a private Christian family life again, which is the priceless boon of every true family.

Second—To give our younger children a better chance for an education and the older ones better opportunities for the development of their educational abilities.

Third—To relieve our wife from the hard work, which she in her advancing years cannot endure.

Fourth—To redeem ourselves from the many worriments and excitements which are connected therewith.

We are a lover of family life, but here we had to give it up entirely. Some institutions like this have a private home for the Superintendent, and this is the right way to do it, if he has a family. It is indeed very sad that these orphans have lost their homes and cannot enjoy the parental care and love, but at the same time it cannot be expected from the Superintendent to raise his children the same way and not to give the older children a better opportunity, if possible, to improve their abilities.

Every mother knows that children cause much work. It is much more so in such a large family like this. And, as we had no cook for over three months, Mrs. Holter had to be matron, cook and nurse, which was too much for her. It would be wrong to have her life shortened by such overwork and make our own children to orphans with such a home.

Many worriments and excitements at the Home, through gossips and slandering of some papers, are connected thereto. It takes strong nerves to stand it long. We both are not physically strong enough for that, therefore we came to the conclusion to give up this work again for the reasons stated.

On New Year's Day, 1909, we start our pastoral work at our new field in Brooklyn, but we shall never forget the Lutheran Orphans' Home at Topton as long as we live. We always shall remember this work in our prayers, and, if we are able to do anything for this institution, we shall do so gladly and willingly.

We wish to thank all our friends for the kind donations they have sent to this Home, especially during the past year. We hope and pray that they will keep on doing so in the future. We also hope and pray that the Board may soon find a suitable man.

We are sorry to say that Rev. A. M. Weber, who had been called, has declined to fill this place. We are sure that God will not forsake His work, but will richly bless it in the future. We wish all our kind readers a very Happy New Year and God's richest blessings forever more.

F. HOLTER

Rev. Adam M. Weber

The final mystery in this short chapter deals with Rev. Adam M. Weber of Boyertown. He was a charter member of the Board of Directors of the Topton Orphans' Home, well educated and admired, and, according to the last paragraph in Rev. Holter's final epistle, was called, but then declined to take the position.

Chapter 6

YEARS OF GROWTH

The Rev. Jonas O. Henry, D.D.
1909-1945

Rev. Henry was getting to be quite well known at the Home. He'd been temporary Superintendent before Rev. Holter came January 1, 1908. He was now Superintendent, having been called back after Rev. Holter left in January, 1909.

One of the most beautiful images of our story concerns the famous 'buggy ride.' Rev. Henry, then the pastor at Trinity Lutheran Church at Topton, was driving his horse and buggy up Peach Avenue (renamed Home Avenue in 1915) and saw a little girl walking up the hill.

He stopped his buggy and asked, "Are you from the Home?" She was, so he gave her a ride to the top. As she got out, she looked over at him and said, "Won't you come up and be our daddy?"

The Rev. J. O. Henry, D.D.

Mrs. Ida Sefing Henry

That night he told his wife, Ida: "I feel the Lord is calling us through this little girl to take charge of this work. If you are willing, we will answer this call." Ida was willing, and on July 1, 1909, Rev. Henry took full charge. It was a job he was destined to fill ably for more than 36 eventful years. It is entirely fitting that his eyes were opened to his REAL calling by a small angel in a little girl's dress.

The Lutheran Orphans' Home enjoyed a remarkable period of expansion during the years when Rev. Henry and his wife directed its destiny. When Rev. Henry took over in 1909, it was only 10 years old. William Howard Taft was in the White House in an America that seemed to be completely isolated from the power politics of Europe where Germany, France and Russia were building huge war machines. The automobile was also about 10 years old, and its influence was beginning to be felt in the land.

In assuming his new charge, Rev. Henry immediately began to plan for much needed expansion. Jacob C. Stotter and his wife, a Pottstown couple, gave a tower clock and bell, and the pealing of this bell for the first time on August 18, 1910, seemed to be a portent of great progress.

Annie L. Lowry Memorial Infirmary

The following year, the estate of Annie L. Lowry underwrote the cost of a new building that was to be known as the

Annie L. Lowry Memorial Infirmary. This two-story structure, erected for the sizeable sum of $5,500 in 1911, served
as the infirmary until 1956, when bed patients were moved
to the infirmary section of the new Caum Memorial Building
in Reading. Today the Annie Lowry Building has been
recycled into offices for the Children's Department.

Pennsylvania's population in 1910 was more than double
that of 1870, and this rapid growth was also reflected in
Berks County, whose population had increased 40,000 since
the idea of the Lutheran Orphans' Home was conceived.
Accordingly, The Orphans' Home's family was growing and
the Trustees turned their attention to the main building,
where the addition of wings to the east and west seemed
entirely feasible. These two-story additions were also completed in 1911 at a cost of $12,500. As we look at the build-
ing today, that pricetag is 'astounding!' These wings provided badly needed space. Suddenly, there were additional
dormitories, school rooms and a chapel.

Administration Building

The chapel, furnished by the Orphans' Home Society of
Reading's Trinity Lutheran Church, was dedicated on May
24, 1911 and immediately assumed an important role in the

Home's religious life.

As we'll see throughout the book, each new building, wing or room became an opportunity for a congregation or family to 'adopt' and make their own special place. Powerful motivators: it was located within easy visiting distance AND it was helping orphans.

Yet there was no "book of rules" for this new institution. The tremendous struggle to make The Lutheran Orphans' Home a reality needed leadership...and got it from the start. These were years of irresistible progress. Momentum seemed to grow daily.

One year after the Annie L. Lowry Infirmary and the wings to the main building became part of the development on the knoll, an addition was built on the dining room section of the main building to provide more dining space for the growing family of dependent children.

Dining Room
(with Rev. Henry serving!)

In 1914, when America was pondering the outcome of the war that had broken out in Europe, the very first infant was admitted.

Up to this time, children under the age of three had not been admitted, but the need to provide care for small babies who had been deprived of a mother's care had been felt for some time.

George E. Holton Memorial Cottage for Infants

The inclusion of infants posed the immediate problem of providing a special building for their care. The Trustees worked on plans and specifications. Mrs. Jessica Holton of Catasauqua, PA provided the funds for the erection and equipping of a babies' cottage.

On June 28, 1916, the building was dedicated as the George E. Holton Memorial Cottage for Infants. In 1962, it became a staff residence. Tower Court now stands there.

ANNIVERSARY DAY TRADITION

While the building program continued to make news throughout the community and in the Lutheran Church of Pennsylvania, life went on at the Orphans' Home.

The first Anniversary Day had been held on August 16, 1900, so it became a tradition that the Lutheran Home's birthday was celebrated each succeeding year on the third Thursday in August, for the convenience of the large number of farmers. Later, it was changed to the last Saturday in July, which was more convenient to those with weekday jobs.

This annual "Day" attracted thousands of friends to Topton to attend the program and make open house tours of the buildings. As the years went by, more and more alumni helped to swell the Anniversary Day crowds.

Health of the children was given a great deal of attention from the start. However, from time to time, the outbreaks of disease sweeping the country would also affect Topton.

In 1916, 41 children affected with scarlet fever were restored to health in the infirmary. In 1920, there were 82 cases of influenza out of 165 children. All recovered. Articles in the Kutztown Patriot tell of the 1919 influenza epidemic;

schools were closed (Dryville school closed for four weeks) and tell that nearly every family representing that school had the disease. Many have forgotten how devastating these epidemics were. Sadly, they had a direct bearing on the Lutheran Orphans' Home.

THE SCHOOL HOUSE

During 1917, a two-story brick school building was erected. It contained four school rooms, a supply room, a dental room and a large room in the basement for manual training. The building, "with modern improvements and equipment" cost $15,000.

Three rooms were opened in September, 1918 and the fourth room was opened in September, 1921 for a Junior High School. A regular music teacher for all the schools was employed in 1919.

RECREATION

Healthy, growing youngsters needed recreational outlets for their youthful energy. Early on, a small dam was built in a grove near the campus. This provided swimming in the summertime and an ice-skating area in the winter months.

In 1911, a cement bathing pool had been built in the main building's basement, through a generous donation by the Band of the Wartburg Orphans' School in Mount Vernon, NY and St. John's German Lutheran Church in Reading. Water for the pool was heated by steam pipes connected to the boiler. A very clever idea!

A wading pool 50´ in diameter constructed in 1916 between the Holton Memorial Cottage and the schoolhouse became a popular gathering place for the smaller youngsters. *(Hm. Seems like the bigger kids also jumped right in!)*

During the Spring of 1919, part of the breast and side of the dam washed away. The Trustees decided to build a new and larger dam. This provided a larger swimming and skating area, plus all the ice needed for the Home. Usually during the month of January, ice was harvested and stored for summer use (see p. 41.)

A rustic pavillion (24´ x 96´) was constructed on the south side of the boys' playground in 1912. It gave the boys a fine place to play in rainy weather, so they could be outside but not get wet. The girls' pavillion (26´ x 36´) was built in 1919.

Various Lutheran Conferences in the synod were helping to face the challenge that The Lutheran Home represented. The Pottsville Conference undertook the task of furnishing all the coal for heating the various buildings and assumed the responsibility for the coal fund.

In the mid-twenties, we were again 'bursting at the seams' as applications for admission of more and more children came to Rev. Henry.

WORLD WAR I

The idyllic isolation of The Lutheran Home was coming to an end, as the United States was becoming a world power and was drawn into World War I. The country was becoming familiar with names of far-off places, black banner war headlines and a "war economy." The Lutheran Home was not removed from this phenomenon. In 1918, 16 of the boys were in the nation's military service. John Aaron and Walter Madenford died in the service.

In 1919, eight of the children passed the Township Examination for entrance into high school. One entered Muhlenberg College. The main building was wired for electric lights.

In 1921, nine of the children were placed into private homes. The generosity of friends enabled three of the children to attend the Normal School at Kutztown, four at the Commercial School at Allentown and one at Muhlenberg College, Allentown.

ALUMNI ASSOCIATION

An organization of the young men and women who spent parts of their lives at the Lutheran Orphans' Home was started on January 1, 1921, with an attendance of 55. On Anniversary Day, August 18, 1921, a bronze tablet was unveiled bearing the names of Walter Madenford and John Aaron, who died while serving in France. A new 80 ft. flag pole was also dedicated by the alumni.

In 1922, an addition of eight rooms, at a cost of $20,000, was built to relieve crowded conditions. Two years later, generous legacies enabled the Board to make long-awaited expansion and to create an endowment fund.

In 1925, all of the children were vaccinated and immunized against an epidemic of diptheria. There was only one fatal case, in 1928. In 1928, the schools were placed under state supervision.

In 1929, ninth, tenth and eleventh grade pupils attended the high schools at Topton and Kutztown. A refrigeration plant was erected on campus.

In the early 1930's, incomes from bequests and contributions shrank considerably, due to the national depression. However, contributions continued sufficient to maintain the status quo. However, the depression caused more hardship, and the number of applicants increased.

By 1934, the Orphans' Home was filled to capacity. Through careful housekeeping, the supply of foodstuffs from congregations, the farms and gardens carried the large family through without running a deficit.

In 1936, we note that three of the girls were taking the

nurses' training course in the Allentown Hospital. One boy was at Muhlenberg College, preparing for the ministry.

Photo courtesy Kenneth Boldt

THE HISTORY OF THE LUTHERAN HOME PUTZ*

The Lutheran Home welcomes you to its annual viewing of the Christmas Putz. For many years, thousands of men, women and children have been fascinated with this panoramic display that spans 560 square feet and includes 17 scenes.

Much of the Putz is a labor of love produced by Mrs. Ida Henry, who was the matron of The Lutheran Home. She and her husband, The Rev. Dr. J. O. Henry, and their three children moved to The Lutheran Home in 1909 when Dr. Henry was named Superintendent.

---

*Author's Note: This is the script used by the narrator. Pretend you're taking a tour of the Putz many years ago!

A Gift of Love

Mrs. Henry was determined to impress upon the orphans in the care of The Lutheran Home the importance of the birth of the Christ Child and the true meaning of Christmas.

A traditional miniature display was quite popular in the area, and Mrs. Henry decided to use her creativity and this tradition to share the Christmas story in this way. Instead of

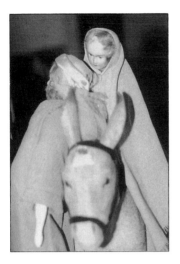

giving personal gifts to every child each year, Mrs. Henry would add something new and different to the Christmas Putz. She continued to enlarge and develop new ideas for this spectacle each year.

Much of the Putz was designed and created by Mrs. Henry through countless hours of patience and intricate work. She started the Putz with the story of the Holy Birth, which is located separately from the secular display in today's Putz. The house where the angel Gabriel visited Mary was built by Mrs. Henry and lined in dark blue velvet.

She dressed the angel in white and Mary in blue. Mary's body is made of a white kid glove so that she would be flexible and could kneel before the angel. Mrs. Henry made both hairpieces, and Mary's is made of human hair.

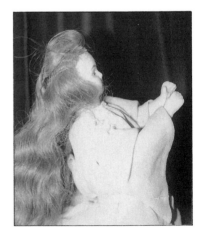

Mrs. Henry also built the Inn and placed the Innkeeper saying "no room" and the cattle in stalls beneath the living quarters. The scene of Christ's birth is portrayed in a larger setting so that the children could better see it. Above the stable is a scene in Bethlehem with a small church to represent the Church of the Nativity which today stands over the place where Christ was born.

The Rev. Theodore Ressler, an orphan raised at The Home, visited the Holy Land and brought from Bethlehem the small bell for Mrs. Henry to place in the steeple of the Church of the Nativity.

The sheep and the angels of the adjacent scene of the shepherd's field were imported from Europe. Many of the angels are handcarved from wood. Mrs. Henry painstakingly dressed the shepherds to resemble their native attire.

The wise men and their camels also had hours of painstaking work in their construction.

On the larger platform of the Putz display, visitors have always delighted in the many secular scenes created by Mrs. Henry. Everything is all set up; with just the flick of 46 switches,

two model railroad trains take their course, a rollercoaster runs on the motor of an old Victrola and a miniature merry-go-round made by Mrs. Henry whirls.

Looking past these and many more moving portions, visitors can see a replica of Radio City Music Hall.

Mrs. Henry, who always had a soft spot in her heart for Radio City, reflected it by recreating the fabulous stage in miniature form for the Putz.

If she had any problem in designing new scenery for the religious pageants, she would go, armed with a box of home-made caramels, to consult with the manager of staging and scenery at Radio City. He would tell her where to go, what to buy, and how to create the scene and then give her the best seat in the house to see the current show.

She used a picture postcard of Radio City as a guide to create the curtains and the steps for the dancers. She recre-ated the hall, complete with the organ to the left of the stage and the orchestra in the pit.

The adjacent amusement park includes trees homemade by Mrs. Henry, and the light in the park are from the origi-nal display. Mrs. Henry built the miniature merry-go-round with its horses and children as well as the cages for all the animals in the nearby zoo. She dressed Snow White and built the small organ upon which Snow White accompanied the dwarfs when they sang while mining.

The replica of the Holton Memorial Cottage, which at one

time housed orphans on the Topton campus, is furnished with miniatures of the period. Photographs of Dr. & Mrs. Henry are seen in the doorway on the cottage porch. Dr. Henry is holding his only grandson.

The cottage and the neighboring church were built by Mrs. Henry. The church has become the most popular portion of the Putz. The interior of the church can be seen through an opening in the roof, and it is decorated for a wedding. The tiny hymnals, baptismal font, and the pipe organ are made of lollipop sticks and lead pencils. The organ stops are small black and white headed pins. The pews are filled with small people. Outside the church, the bridal party is leaving. The windows are covered with figured paper and painted with spermaceti, an oily wax, to make them transparent, creating the effect of stained glass when the light shines through.

The circus tent with bleachers located in the middle of the secular portion of the Putz is the last item made by Mrs. Henry before she and Dr. Henry retired after serving the home for almost 37 years.

The Herald

The War years came and went. Once again, letters with foreign postmarks were quoted in The Herald, as sons and daughters went off to war. The Lutheran Home continued to grow. More and more friends were regular readers of The Herald, the monthly publication of the Home. Back in 1896, one of the first duties of the Superintendent by the Board of Trustees was..."to publish the Orphans' Home Paper monthly and distribute it among the people, so that they may be kept informed and thereby become interested."

The first copy of the Orphans' Home Paper was issued in January 1897, and its influence and popularity have increased through the years. In 1940, it gained a magazine format and color was added. In 1959, The Herald became bi-monthly. It is now a two-color tabloid-size publication, full of photos and articles on the many aspects of the mission.

The number of visitors to a growing group of buildings rising above the borough increased each year. Administering the business of The Lutheran Home was becoming a tremendous task. Fortunately, the Henrys were more than equal to the challenge.

DOWN ON THE FARM

During the summer months, the children helped on the farm and in the gardens. An early photograph shows older boys working in the 'truck patch' picking peas . Look at the HUGE baskets to fill! Everyone's got a good straw hat...and the man at the right is dressed in a long sleeved shirt AND a vest! (And we complain if the air conditioning isn't quite cool enough!)

The other nine months of the year, school sessions were held. At the end of each year, the County Superintendent of Schools gave the boys and girls Township Examinations. The excellent work of the Home's School is evident in the record of how many boys and girls went on to higher levels at colleges and State Normal Schools.

The 1920 church census showed that the number of Lutherans in Berks County had grown to 33,000 confirmed members and more than 50,000 baptized members. They, as well as Lutherans outside the county and people of all faiths, were taking increasing pride in the ever-expanding Orphan's Home.

The years historians refer to as the 'roaring twenties' were a period of quiet progress here. As the century entered its third decade, the orphans family included 165 children housed in the original Main Building and the Infant's cottage. In addition to the farm structures, the schoolhouse and Annie L. Lowry Infirmary also graced the campus on the knoll overlooking Topton Borough.

NEW BUILDINGS

The Allentown Conference, when made aware of the problem of insufficient space, rose to the occasion and pledged a sum to erect a Boy's Cottage.

In 1926, this much-needed building was built

Junior Boys' Allentown Conference Cottage

at a cost of $35,000, making it the most costly structure on the campus to that time. Four years later, when accommodations for girls were urgently needed, a new girls' cottage was erected. This building, with a depression year price-tag of $29,999 was a real Godsend, as support necessarily decreased in the lean years of the thirties.

Junior Girls' Cottage (became Kehl-Charles Memorial Cottage for Girls)

In 1944, this unit became known as the Kehl-Charles Memorial Cottage for Girls, named in memory of the parents of Dr. & Mrs. George W. Kehl of Reading, whose generous bequest reimbursed the Home for the original cost of the cottage. It was later razed to make room for Tower Court apartments.

In 1934, the Reading Conference Luther League presented the children with a gift that was to play a lasting role in their recreation and training. It was the large outdoor swimming pool that served as a focal point of summer fun and where the youngsters were taught swimming and water safety skills. After the orphans were gone, the pool was razed for new buildings.

ADDITIONAL ACREAGE

Just as the number of buildings was growing, the property lines had been expanding through the years. In 1905, the nine-acre Weida property had been added to the 105-acre Peter Diener farm that had been purchased as the original plot in 1896.

The Butz farm, boasting 156 acres, became available and was purchased in 1923, a move that more than doubled the Home's real estate.

A year later, the 29-acre Bieber tract was acquired; it is the location of the Shomo Memorial Water Supply. Twenty-seven additional acres were given to the Home by F.M. Miller in 1941. Additional acreage brings the total to 420.

The year 1939 concluded a decade of change and turbulence in America and throughout the world. Emerging from a great economic depression was the grim spectre of war, as the dictators of Europe and Asia, gaining confidence from each diplomatic victory, rattled their sabers.

The Lutheran Home, having weathered the depression's storm, would soon be sending its sons and daughters off to service in "The Big One", World War II.

HENRY BUILDING

Despite the gathering war clouds, 1939 was a year the Lutheran Orphans' Home would never forget. The Rev. Jonas O. Henry, D.D. and his devoted wife, Ida were celebrating their 30th anniversary of tireless service as Superintendent and Matron. Congratulatory messages from alumni and friends in all parts of the nation clogged the tiny Topton post office. How often we hear it said when a memorial is dedicated: "I wish he could have been here to see it." The Trustees stilled such regrets when they agreed to name the new school and recreation building the "Henry Building." On May 17, 1939, this $92,000 structure was dedicated in honor of the pastor and his wife. The Henry Building, long needed on the campus, had a large auditorium that was ideal for entertainment, plays and pageants. It could quickly be converted to a gymnasium for basketball and other indoor sports. There were seven classrooms in the building as well as a library and dental room. The basement included a large dining room and kitchen. This was a fitting tribute to the couple who devoted the better part of their lifetime to 'providing for them.'

The October, 1944 issue of <u>The Herald</u> lists a full page of Alumni in the service of their country.

★ ★ ★ ★ ★ ★ ★ ★ ★ ★ ★ ★ ★ ★ ★

ALUMNI MEMBERS IN THE SERVICE

Whose Addresses We Have

Lt. Col. Margaret E. Aaron N. 700828, Bruns General Hospital, Santa Fe, New Mexico.

Pfc. William Baer, Battery C. 588 A. A. A. (A.W.) Bn. Camp Hulen, Texas.

Cpl. Earl A. Bagenstose 33187657, 98th Service Sqdn. A.P.O. 638 83rd Service Gp. c/o P.M. New York, N. Y.

T/S Francis Boldt 6886159, Battery D. 380th A.A.A.A.W. Bn. Camp Haan, Cal.

Pfc. Kenneth Boldt 936073, Service Sqdn. M.A.G. 52 9th M.A.W., Congaree Field, Columbia, S. C.

Arthur Challinor S 1/c U.S.S.. Viego 3rd Div. c/o F.P.O. San Francisco, Cal.

Pvt. Robert Daniels 33612544, A.P. 3 F.A.R.T.C. Fort Bragg, N. C.

Pvt. Howard G. Falk A. S., I.—M—11 —W—14 Naval Air Station 55, Jacksonville, Fla.

Pvt. William D. Falls U.S.M.C. 26th Provisional Co. 5th Defense Btn. Reinforced F.P.O. San Francisco, Cal.

Cpl. George J. Fisher 33489861, Btry C. 331st F. A. Bn. A.P.O. 450 E.R.R. Cl. 65. Camp Cooke, Cal.

Pfc. Jacob A. Fisher 33833152, C.C. Adm. Hq. Box No. 68 A.A.B. North Area, Alamogordo, New Mexico.

Sgt. Luther G. Frick. 35th Technical School Squadron, Chanute Field, Ill.

P. F. German A.S. 2/c, 33rd Spec. Plt. 3 A.B.D., Camp Rousseau, Cal.

William German S 2/c, U.S.S. P. C. 1204, c/o F.P.O., New York, N. Y.

Pvt. Frederick Gruhler, Btry. D. 216th C.A. (A. A.) San Francisco, Cal.

M/Sgt. Geary Gum 12004769, 315th Sig Co., Bomb Div. A.P.O. 558. c/o P.M., New York, N. Y.

Pvt. John Gum 33617630 A.S.N., H. 2 Co. 2 Bn. 187th Inf., Glider, A.P.O. 468, c/o P.M., San Francisco, Cal.

Elvin R. Hartman S. F. 3/c, U.S. Naval Hospital, San Diego, Cal.

John M. Hafner S 1/c, U.S.N. No. 147. Box F. c/o F.P.O., New York, N. Y.

Sgt. Richard Hecker 13050568 7th Comm. Sqdn. A.P.O. 304. c/o P.M. Bend, Oregon.

Lawrence N. Heffner 33230145. Co. B. 843rd Sig. Ser. Bn. A.P.O. 702. c/o P.M., Minneapolis, Minnesota.

Burton Hilliard, Seaman's Ch. Institute, 25 South St., Box 935, New York, N. Y.

Jacob Holtry S 2/c, U.S.S.S.C. 1242 Fleet P.O., New York, N. Y.

Harvey Hottle S 2/c, Hospital Corps School (84-6), Norfolk Naval Hospital, Portsmouth, Va.

Pfc. Lester Hottle, 558 Service Sudn. 43rd Ser. Gn. A.P.O. 520. c/o P.M., New York, N. Y.

William Huey, Naval Training Station, Newport, R. I.

Pvt. Robert F. Hughes, Jr., A.S.N. 39564001 69th Depot Repair Sqdn. South Kelly Field, Texas.

Pvt. Earl J. F. Huyer A.S.N. 33055821. 92nd Machine Records Unit, Fort Knox, Ky.

2nd Lt. Betty Jean Kleckner A.N.C.N. 760332. 7th Gen. Hospital. A.P.O. 507. c/o P.M., New York, N. Y.

William Klein A.S. 1/c, c/o Fleet P.O., U.S.S. Picking, San Francisco, Cal.

Cpl. George F. Klinger 33489622, Co. C. 1299 Engrs. Combat Bn., Camp Bowie, Texas.

Klotz, Pvt. Melvin 33836418, Co. A. 3188 Sig. S.V. Bn., Fort Monmouth, N. J.

Pvt. Ellwood H. Lahr 33835689, Inf. Co. I. A.P.O. 15377. c/o P.M., New York, N. Y.

Pfc. Woodrow D. Lahr 13046488. A.P.O. 710, 1011th Sig Co. (Av'n) Serv. Gp., c/o P.M., San Francisco, Cal.

Pvt. Calvin Laudenslager 33505059, 1145th M.P. Co., (Av'n), A.P.O. 636. Det. A., c/o P.M., New York, N. Y.

Cpl. George Laudenslager 13046491, 21st Troop Carrier Sqdn. A.P.O. 923, c/o P.M, San Francisco, Cal.

Pvt. Arnold Lotz 33354559, Med. Det. 203rd Gen. Hos. A.P.O. 645, c/o P.M., New York, N. Y.

Pvt. Paul Machajdik, U.S.S. Colorado, Box 9, c/o P.M., San Francisco, Cal.

Pvt. Harold Miller, Reg. 6359, Veterans Administration Hos., Lyons, N. J.

Pfc. Herman Miller, 49th Ord. So. (M.M.) 13th Ord. Br. A.P.O. No. 9401, San Francisco, Cal.

Pfc. Willard Miller 33365741, Co. I, 22nd Inf., A.P.O. 4, c/o P.M., New York, N. Y.

Sgt. Arthur B. Moyer, 322nd Inf. Ser. Co., A.P.O. 81, c/o P.M., San Francisco, Cal.

Pfc. Samuel O. Mummey, S.S. 34 M.A.G. 34 M.C.A.S. F.M.F., Cherry Point, N. C.

J. Kenneth Naus F. 1/c, U.S.S. Macomb, c/o F.P.O., New York, N. Y.

E. Paul Painter A.S., Texas Transport & Terminal, c/o F.P.O., Corpus Christi, Texas.

Sgt. Sterling Painter 33013008, Co. F. 12th Inf., Tilton Gn. Hospital, Fort Dix, N. J.

Pvt. John Perschau 6075193, Btty D. 252nd Coast Artillery. A.P.O. 880, c/o P.M., New York, N. Y.

Pvt. Robert Perschau 6847947, Hq. Btry 559 F. A. Bn. A.P.O. 308, c/o P.M., New York, N. Y.

Pvt. Emil Rash, Pearl Harbor Hospital, Pearl Harbor, Hawaii.

A. B. Walter Rash, Seaman's Institute. Box 1544, 25 South St., New York, N. Y.

Orville Reich A.S. Commanding Officer, U.S. Coast Guard Naval Station, Fort McHenry, Baltimore, Md.

Pvt. Henry Reidnauer A.S.P.D, H. 2 Co., Camp Reynolds, U.S. Army P.O. Greenville, Pa.

Pfc. Thomas Reidnauer A.S.N. 33316,-666, Sec. A., Platoon 3, Ellington Field, Texas.

Pvt. Roland Reiter 33836237, Med. Det. 407 Inf. A.P.O. 102, Fort Dix, N. J.

Sgt. Donald R. Schaeffer, 353rd Replacement Co, A.P.O. 67, c/o P.M., New York, N. Y.

Clair S. Shurr, S 2/c, Basic Engineers, Phib. T.B., Ft. Pierce, Fla.

Luther Silfies, A.S., Co. 1822, U. S. Naval T.S., Great Lakes, Ill.

Paul F. Silfies S 1/c, Hdqts. Co., Section II, 8th Spec. Battalion, c/o F.P.O., San Francisco, Cal.

Robert Silfies M. M. 3/c, U.S.S. Franklin, Division M., c/o F.P.O., San Francisco, Cal.

Pfc. William F. Smith 33011413, Co. B., 38th Engineers, A.P.O. 622, c/o P.M., Miami, Fla.

Leander Weiss, S.M. 3/c, L.C.T. 133, Navy 225, c/o F.P.O., San Francisco, Cal.

Sgt. Chester Werst, Coast Artillery, Battery B., c/o P.M., Staten Island, N. Y.

Pfc. Russell H. Werst 33114713, Section C., Flight C, R.A.A.F., Roswell, New Mexico.

Cpl. Vincent Wertman A.S.N. 33618025 54th Fighter Group, 54th Fighter Sqdn., Bartow Army Air Base, Bartow, Fla.

Pvt. Winfred R. Wertman 33493661, Co. M., 22nd Inf. A.P.O. 4, c/o P. M., New York, N. Y.

Pvt. Raymond O. Wetherich 33831096, Co. A., 82nd Bn., Camp Fannin, Texas.

Richard P. Wilson, S. 1/c, Brks. No. 15, U.S. Naval Air Station, Ottumwa, Iowa.

Cpl. Anna Yanchurek, Wac., 4802 Roland Ave., Baltimore 10, Md.

Two were honorably discharged and two killed in action.

There are others not on this list for want of their correct addresses.

★ ★ ★ ★ ★ ★ ★ ★ ★ ★ ★ ★ ★ ★ ★

**Part of the crowd at the 1946 Anniversary Day--
the first held since pre-World War II days.**

REV. RAKER'S LEGACY

At the time of his resignation as Superintendent in 1907, the Rev. John H. Raker, D.D. had raised a sum of $5,500 for a proposed Old Folks' Home at Topton. While this special fund was held in escrow though the years, this idea of the far-seeing Dr. Raker received only fleeting attention.

However, as the thirties drew to a close, the Board of Trustees fully recognized that the care of the aged was a real and growing problem that would have to be faced as soon as possible.

1940 became a great year of decision. While the so-called 'phony' war became a real conflict when Hitler overran most of Europe and Japan extended its 'co-prosperity sphere' at bayonet point through more and more of the orient, the Home's Trustees grappled with the task of making changes to meet the great need of the mid-century.

NEW IDENTITY, LARGER BOARD

In 1896, it was named "The Lutheran Orphan's Home in Berks County, Pennsylvania." Now it became the more inclusive title, "The Lutheran Home at Topton, Pennsylvania." The Lutheran Home, thereby, was able to provide for the elderly, plus other services, not just orphans.

In advocating a twofold program, the Trustees recognized that their Board no longer was large enough to provide effective leadership and direction. Synodical approval was duly given to enlarge the Board from 12 to 18 members, including six representatives from the Ministerium of Pennsylvania.

The corporate body from the Reading Conference area chose the other 12, with membership evenly divided between clergy and laity. Since the inception of the Orphan's Home, its publication had been called "The Orphan's Home Paper." It became "The Herald of the Lutheran Home at Topton" on Dec. 10, 1940.

AGING SERVICES BEGIN

Services to the aging began officially on Nov. 12 of that year, when the Trustees solemnly authorized the use of the Annie Lowry Building. A month later, this cottage was ready for 10 aged guests. On May 13, Mrs. Fyanna Flicker of Dryville, Berks County, became the first guest. She was 79.

Here are excerpts from an explanatory article:

Aug. 1941 - WHAT ABOUT THE HOME FOR THE AGED?

The present arrangement for the aged is only temporary. The Annie Lowry Memorial is to take care of the sick. For years it was not needed for sick, for which we are deeply grateful. On account of the many appeals for help, it was decided to use the Annie Lowry Memorial until a building can be erected and specially equipped for aged residents.

Many Homes for the aged have been visited by members

of the board, staff and architects to study plans of buildings and equipment. Architects Ritcher and Eiler have made a study of such homes. Their firm is preparing drawings for the proposed building. After all plans and specifications are completed, they must be submitted to proper state authorities for their study and approval.

We selected the building site and are working on plans for the building. However, before we can go ahead with the erection of the building, there are a few very important matters to be considered carefully.

A building to meet the needs of the aged must not only be carefully planned but also properly equipped. Such a building costs considerable money. To meet the payments of such a building is the important thing, and the want of the funds needed, is the reason why we are not building.

The need is great, the site selected, the architects working on plans, the board of trustees anxious to build and meet the need for the aged; who will help to provide the funds necessary?

Think it over and see what you can do. If necessary, and you deem it advisable, we shall be pleased to meet with you at any time and at any place you may suggest, for a more detailed study of the need and how to meet it.

Your suggestions, as well as those of your friends, are welcomed. Think of it, talk of it, work for it, ask the Lord to guide us. By working together with God and our means we shall succeed.

Pay us a visit at your leisure. We shall be pleased to show you the proposed site of the building and the plans to date. Think, dear friend, of how much good you can do and how much joy and comfort you can give to the needy aged. There is surely a real need.

To assist in the expanded program, the Rev. Paul J. Henry was called from his parish in Ephrata, PA to work with his father. The younger Rev. Henry served as assistant superintendent until 1946, when he was called to the pastorate of Grace Church in Royersford, PA.

WORLD WAR II

The Trustees were anxious to go ahead with plans for another building for the aged, but the events of December 7, 1941 and the months that followed made this impossible. It was already apparent that a building for 50 old people would not really be adequate in view of the admission requests that Dr. Henry was receiving. While only ten aged guests were in care, 180 children were here, and as high school classes graduated, some boys and a few girls would go off to war.

Whether in Georgia, California, Sicily, Iwo Jima or Burma, the servicemen knew that the prayers of the Henrys and all those at the Home were always with them.

HENRY ANNOUNCES RETIREMENT

Late in 1945, Dr. Henry announced that he and his wife would retire at the end of that year. Not many could remember when the Henrys had NOT been in charge.

Dr. Henry explained that the long stewardship had taken a certain toll and it was time to turn over the reins to a younger man. As the bells of New Year's Eve rang out the old, they also heralded the end of an era in this proud history.

Dr. & Mrs. Henry lived in retirement in Allentown until his death on May 15, 1955. His widow later became a guest at the Caum Memorial, Reading, until her death in 1964.

Many words have been written about the contribution the Henrys made to The Lutheran Home at Topton. The Henry Building stands as a small token of appreciation for their untiring efforts.

In 1949, Miss Mary E. Belser, a member of the staff, presented a tower music system dedicated in honor of Dr. & Mrs. Henry, who saw the institution grow from just one incomplete building to a group of six buildings plus other facilities.

MARY E. BELSER

This chapter would not be complete without a tribute to Mary E. Belser, identified with The Lutheran Home at Topton for an incredible 48 years. She was Office Manager, then Secretary to the Superintendent. Her service began in Dr. Henry's tenure and lasted through Rev. Reinert's years.

The following are excerpts from Rev. Reinert's **In Memoriam** of December, 1974.

Her service began in 1926, after five years as a first-grade teacher in the Bethlehem, PA School District. She joined shortly after visiting here with a group from St. Mark's Lutheran Church in Bethlehem. She taught fifth and sixth grades, then combined first and second grades for 19 years.

No one worked in the office at that time, so after finishing her teaching (and on weekends) Miss Belser did office work. She had dreamed of missionary work, but an emergency here changed her view.

A diphtheria epidemic broke out and the infirmary had an instant overload of patients. Then the entire nursing staff got a reaction from the diphtheria inoculations and Miss Belser was a 'nurse' for a full week. "That's when I realized that there was probably as much 'missionary' work for me here, so I gave up my idea of foreign service."

During the years when it was customary to take groups of children from the Home family to supporting congregations, Miss Belser directed the program. These contacts with thousands of friends of the Topton Home identified Miss Belser as one of the best public relations persons ever.

She was our statistician, had facts and figures at her fingertips and regularly prepared statistical monthly and annual reports. She was our "human computer" and could gather and relay office information at a moment's notice.

Only when she was gone did we realize the incredible amount of things she accomplished by herself.

She managed the office, recorded cash contributions, wrote letters of thanks all the time. She kept up the mailing list, prepared copy for <u>The Herald</u> and mailed it out to over 6,000 persons.

Miss Belser at the fascinating Christmas Putz

She was an enthusiastic promoter of our unusual Christmas Putz during the Christmas season (and helped put it up, take it down and store it each year.) She showed it to visitors and narrated the Christmas story as they watched the scenes come to life.

She was a member of the Church Council, sang in the Choir of the Home congregation and took an active part in auxiliary organizations of our Grace congregation and of the Topton Home. Her interest in her flower garden was well-known by the thousands of visitors who saw her flower arrangements in reception rooms, lounges, dining rooms, Chapel and Auditorium.

Here was a dedicated servant of the Church. She was not a trained deaconess set apart for the diaconate, but in many respects she measured up to such a high calling in the social ministry of the Church.

She was helpful in making the transition from one administration to another, and since January 1946 to the time of her death served as secretary to the present Superintendent.

Chapter 7

TRANSITION YEARS

The Rev. Webster K. Reinert, D.D.
1946-1975

Rev. Webster K. Reinert, the new Superintendent, had been pastor of Grace Lutheran Church in Phillipsburg, NJ for 14 years, having answered that call following his ordination. In a sense, he was coming 'home' when he came to Topton, as he had been born in Oley, just a few miles down the road.

His schooling was at Keystone State Normal at Kutztown; Muhlenberg College, Allentown and Mt. Airy Seminary in

The Rev. Webster K. Reinert
Superintendent

Mrs. Mary Reinert
Matron

Philadelphia, PA, where he graduated in 1932. Rev. & Mrs. Mary Reinert both had been confirmed in the Amityville Parish, where Rev. Heilman had been Pastor when **he** was called to be the first Superintendent.

On January 16, 1946, the Reinerts and their three children arrived. In care were 175 children and 12 old people. Conditions were crowded. The staff was small. Five years earlier, the Annie Lowry Infirmary had been converted to a cottage for old people, but World War II had halted plans to increase facilities for the aged.

This steel engraving, about 50 years old, shows "Old Main" in 1909 and 1945.

Still on the drawing board was a large unit to house over 100 elderly. Facilities for 50 guests were to be built as soon as possible, with an equal amount to follow. Lack of funds prevented any action. The Trustees were beginning to question the advisability of large buildings as units for group care of children OR the elderly.

Rev. Reinert was installed on April 28, 1946 by the Rev. Emil E. Fisher, D.D., President of the Ministerium of Pennsylvania. It was already apparent that the new Superintendent was a serious student of the problem of group care. Times had changed. Methods and techniques that had been popular and effective in caring for children and old people had become outmoded. The Trustees were happy to see that Rev. Reinert kept pace with social progress.

Krum Memorial Cottage (first used as Reinert residence)

In 1949, an attractive and homelike residence for the Reinert family was built, through a bequest from Mrs. Ida A. Krum of Weissport, PA in memory of her son, Dr. Charles P. Krum of Lebanon, PA. The eight-room cottage was dedicated on Jan. 10, 1950 as the "Krum Memorial Cottage." It was the first of many units which were to be built in the Reinert era.

On the southwest end of the Home's campus was a fine building; the residence of Oliver C. Collins, a well-to-do rug manufacturer, with mills in Topton, Hancock and Red Hill.

Heilman Cottage for Old Folks

His widow put the home up for sale after his death in 1949. The Lutheran Home purchased it for $40,000 and spent another $40,000 converting it to a cottage for old folks. On Sept. 17, 1950, the new unit, housing 17 elderly guests, was dedicated as the Heilman Cottage for Old Folks, in memory of the first Superintendent, Rev. U.P. Heilman.

Rev. Reinert was an outspoken advocate of the addition of a case worker. He stressed the need for more intensive work with families to screen children and the need to work more closely with children in care.

Follow-up after the child was released from the Home was another area in which much could be accomplished. In November 1951, the Trustees approved the assignment of a case worker to Topton under the supervision of the Lutheran Children's Bureau in Philadelphia. Miss Catherine

Schmidt of Philadelphia was appointed and was soon doing yeoman work on behalf of the children at the Home.

The opening of the Heilman Cottage for Old People in Sept. 1950 enabled The Lutheran Home to more than double its number of aged in care, to 29. The Trustees realized that this was only the beginning of a program of expansion necessary to meet the ever-growing need of more facilities for those in the golden age of life. The acquisition of the Heilman Cottage was tacit evidence of the abandonment of plans for a large building for old people. From now on, the course would be to build or acquire smaller units for this type of care.

As originally conceived, the so-called "orphan's home" was a refuge for parentless children. There they would live in a group until they finished high school and were old enough to go out into the world. By the middle of the 20th Century, those concerned with child care were well aware that there were far fewer orphans than there had been during the earlier decades.

Children were now being admitted because of broken homes, mental disturbances of parent or parents and a variety of other problems. This changing picture meant a new and different approach to the problem of caring for dependent youngsters.

In addition to the case worker, the staff was increased as the idea of houseparents came into fruition. By employing married couples as house parents, The Lutheran Home could give children the benefits of a family-like situation. All children need parents or parent-figures; houseparents fill that need. Houseparents Mr. & Mrs. Robert Fisher, shown below, represent the vitally needed stable family leadership.

The children, many of whom came from unstable and insecure homes, now had the thing they needed more; guidance and love from mature, secure individuals.

These boys and girls were not the same 'orphans' of yesteryear. Their problems required a great deal more study and attention. This revised program marked the beginning of a new era in group care here.

As the facilities expanded, basic parts of the 'plant' became outmoded. This meant necessary improvements and great sums of money. The tight clay soil of the Topton area provided poor seepage for the cesspools and septic tanks that served for the first 50 years. In 1952, the Trustees approved the building of a sewage treatment plant and sanitary collecting system. A bio-chemical sewage treatment system, the first of its kind in Pennsylvania, was installed. Planned to serve a maximum of 800 persons, the plant cost $70,633 and the collecting system an additional $50,615.

Since the Heilman Cottage is at a lower level on the grounds, a pump house costing $35,237 had to be built. A storm sewer collecting system for surface water drainage on the campus was installed. The total cost of this project was the staggering sum of $153,078.

Other improvements were also in order. The construction of a utility building was begun. This structure, named for H. H. Gilbert of Reading, was built on two levels and housed rest room facilities for visitors, a maintenance shop and much needed storage space. The H. H. Gilbert Memorial, an $81,000 building, proved to be a welcome addition to the campus.

The outmoded electrical distribution system was the next project. Lines were consolidated and a meter room was installed in the sewage disposal plant at a cost of $15,157.

At this time, 35 boys, aged 10 to 18 years, were living in one group in the Main Building. The Trustees agreed with Rev. Reinert that this was too wide an age range. Plans were made to provide separate quarters for the older boys. Because the orphans attended local schools, the old school building had not been used since 1939, except for storage. The building was structurally sound.

The architects advised that it could be remodeled to serve as an excellent boys' unit. On Anniversary Day, August 12,

1954, 20 older boys moved from the Main building into their new home. It was designated as "The Memorial Cottage for Boys." It proved to be a fine home for the older boys.

The new Memorial Cottage for Boys was dedicated on August 12, 1954. The children's family was divided into the following additional groups: baby, small boys, intermediate girls and older girls.

These groups were housed in the George E. Holton Baby

Cottage, the Allentown Conference Cottage for Boys, the Kehl-Charles Memorial for Girls, the Main building and now the new cottage for the older boys. This would be the pattern of children's care for some time to come.

At each month's meeting, the Board of Trustees continued to approve applicants for the aged people's cottages, but, since there was no room in the two units, the Heilman Cottage and Annie Lowry Cottage, the waiting list continued to grow. The acquisition of the Heilman Cottage in 1950, and the success of its conversion into an old people's building, gave the Trustees considerable food for thought.

CAUM MEMORIAL HOME

The Trustees had abandoned the idea of building a large multi-story unit for the aged on the Topton campus for the present. Instead, they hoped to purchase an existing building with conversion possibilities. This would be a quick and economical means of meeting the problem of care for those in the golden years.

When Mrs. Elizabeth B. Caum died in Bethlehem, PA in 1947, she left The Lutheran Home the residue of her estate, the magnificent sum of over $145,976. This sum, designated for use in expanding the program for aged people, was the largest bequest the Home ever received for this work, up to that time. Since her death, it had been held in trust until that day when it could be used in the expansion program.

In their search for a suitable structure, the Trustees kept returning to a famous mansion for sale in the fashionable Hampden Heights section of Reading, PA. It was owned by the Bitting family, wealthy Reading hosiery mill owners.

The property, at 1711 Hampden Boulevard, occupied a full city block. The residency faced Hampden Boulevard. Built of Chestnut Hill stone some 30 years before, the two main stories contained a huge living room, library, large dining room, kitchen, six large bedrooms, solarium, plus several baths. The third floor, used for storage, had expansion possibilities.

Early in 1955, the Trustees purchased the property for

Caum Memorial Home,
Reading, PA

$150,000. Howard I. Eiler, Reading architect, was asked to prepare plans and specifications for the conversion of the structure into a Home for both ambulatory and infirmary guests. The Trustees learned that redesigning the building would add another $150,000. Time proved that this was money well spent.

The kitchen needed additional equipment. The library was removed so it could also serve as a chapel. The living room and dining room needed no changes. The large second floor bedrooms were converted into infirmary rooms, each big enough to contain four hospital beds. A nurse's station was constructed in the hall. The big change was made on the third floor where 11 rooms for ambulatory guests were created. Of course, an elevator had to be installed to serve the basement and three floors.

A song service in the
magnificent Caum living room

A hardy
group poses
by the sign

The renovated structure was opened in December, 1955. The first guest was Miss Rose Dillman, who was transferred from the Annie Lowry Cottage at Topton. The 22 hospital beds and 15 beds for ambulatory guests were quickly filled.

On April 8, 1956, the building was dedicated as the Caum Memorial of The Lutheran Home at Topton, in memory of Mrs. Caum, whose generosity and thoughtfulness had made it possible.

With the addition of the Caum Memorial, The Lutheran Home's old people's family numbered 63. The Heilman Cottage had 17 guests, there were nine in the Annie Lowry Cottage and now 37 in the new Caum Memorial. While real progress had been made in the 15 years since the inception of services for the aged, the waiting list continued to grow.

When all the rooms and infirmary beds were filled in the Caum Memorial for Old People in Reading, the program of care had entered a new and more challenging era. Applications from elderly men and women continued to increase.

One of the reasons was the Caum Memorial building in Reading itself. This location brought the work of the Home to the attention of many city dwellers who weren't familiar with The Lutheran Home's new emphasis. In view of the requests for admission, the Board of Trustees was faced with the problem of again providing for expansion of facilities for those in the golden years of life.

CHAPEL RENOVATION

The basic philosophy of The Lutheran Home had always been to provide for the spiritual as well as temporal needs of the children and old people in its care. For several years, it had become increasingly apparent that the Chapel in the Main Building at Topton was very much in need of modernizing and renovation.

Once an attractive part of the facilities, it had become drab and cheerless over the years. The Trustees approved a complete facelift for this little church where the boys, girls and elderly guests came to pray and worship.

The improvements cost $35,000, making the chapel one of the most attractive spots on the campus. The renovations included replastering, installation of an acoustical tile ceiling, new light fixtures, carpeting, furnishings and windows.

Generous donations from friends enhanced the beauty of the new Chapel. All ten stained-glass windows were contributed as memorials, one being donated by the Alumni Association. Trustee Charles K. Emhardt and his wife, of Hamburg, PA, provided the altar. The pulpit was given by the Dorcas Societies of St. Paul Lutheran Church, Athol, PA, and of Friedens Lutheran, Oley, PA, in honor of the Superintendent and Matron, Rev. and Mrs. W. K. Reinert.

The lectern, baptismal font, communion rail, altar set, missal stand, offering plates, prayer desk kneeler, credence table, hymnboards, flower stands, carpet, clergy seat, choir pews, choir screen, flags, stained-glass doors, nave lights, pews and service books and hymnals all were made possible through the generosity of many friends and patrons of The Lutheran Home.

The new Chapel was formally dedicated on Sunday, October 12, 1958. The Rev. Carlton L. Heckman, S.T.M., pastor of Trinity Lutheran Church, Kutztown, and dean of the Kutztown District of the Ministerium of Pennsylvania, delivered the sermon. Three generous grants from the Henry Janssen Foundation, Reading, helped to make the new 150-seat Chapel a reality.

Rev. & Mrs. Reinert (as pastor and organist/choir director) provided weekly worship services throughout the year. They also broadcast the Sunday services to the Infirmary patients. Rev. Reinert had regular communion for patients in the Henry Infirmary and the Caum Home residents.

Just as the Chapel project was completed, a substantial bequest to The Lutheran Home made possible new plans for expanding the facilities for old people. Mrs. Helen E. Howell, late of Easton, PA, and her sister, Miss Mae S. Unangst, Nazareth, PA, donated a sum that would permit the Trustees to build an addition to the Caum Memorial.

As a memorial to the parents of Mrs. Howell and Miss Unangst, the addition was to be known as the Unangst Memorial Infirmary; 12 rooms for infirmary guests. By the end of 1959 , the new building was completed. Two months later, the first of the 12 new elderly guests was admitted.

The Unangst Infirmary was dedicated on June 26, 1960.

The year 1962 is significant in The Lutheran Home's history of growth and progress, as it marked the completion of one major expansion project and the start of another.

When the Brandywine Heights Joint School District opened a large, new elementary school building in close proximity to The Lutheran Home, it became apparent that the Henry School Building on the campus would no longer be required for the education of our children. At the same time, the need for additional facilities to care for the aged continued to grow. The Board of Trustees, therefore, approved plans for the renovation of the former classroom wing of the Henry Building into a modern infirmary for aged guests.

Construction began in the fall of 1961 and renovations were completed in time for dedication on August 11, 1962, our 65th Anniversary Day. The Henry Infirmary made available accommodations for an additional 41 senior guests, the first of whom were admitted to care on Sept. 1, 1962.

A Lutheran clergyman, who was born at Topton and spent all of his formative years there, returned to assume a considerable responsibility. Rev. Paul J. Henry, D.D., was elected Secretary of the Board of Trustees in June, 1962, when the Rev. Horace S. Mann, who had held the office for 31 years, declined another term.

That Spring, the Board also confirmed the appointment of its first controller, Milton P. Silliman of Allentown. Mr. Silliman, well-qualified through long experience in the retail and insurance fields, was also a very active Lutheran layman. As controller, he became responsible for a wide variety of financial administrative duties.

LUTHER HAVEN

Early in 1962, the Trustees approved a bold new program; a totally different approach to care of the elderly. According to this so-called "cottage plan", The Lutheran Home would erect single-family dwelling units along Home Avenue, in the attractive area north of the Main Building.

Luther Haven

The occupants of these cottages enjoy all the comforts and privacy of their own homes. They cook, keep house and care for themselves as long as they are able. They also have a peace of mind and security because of the Home's nearby facilities and services, which are readily available to them whenever needed.

Three sample cottages were erected and, on October 15, 1962, Rev. Rufus E. Kern and his wife became the first "cottage plan" occupants. Dr. Kern, a retired Lutheran minister, was a long-time member of the Board of Trustees.

"We have all the advantages of living independently in our own home, with our own furnishings," he observed, "yet we are secure in the knowledge that all of the Home's facilities are nearby and available."

The year 1962 also saw the completion of the kitchen renovation. Roger Wentling, who assumed the post of Food Service Manager that Fall, pointed out that the biggest hotels and restaurants could not boast more modern and efficient equipment. The dietary problems of patients in the Henry Infirmary dictated the need for updated kitchen facilities.

ACTIVITIES

The Lutheran Home was not only keeping pace in terms of bricks and mortar. With the increase in the number of aging residents, the need for more creative activities for the guests also became apparent. Craft activities were promoted by Mrs. Carlton L. Heckman, the former Marian Kauffman Henry, who was added to the staff on a part-time basis. The arts and crafts program was soon extended by Mrs. Heckman to include the residents of the Caum Memorial at Reading. Mrs. Denton A. Steffy of West Lawn later became the craft instructor for the guests at The Lutheran Home's extension—the Caum Memorial.

Early in 1963, a program of occupational therapy was created for guests in the Henry Infirmary. Mrs. Sherwood Miller of Kutztown conducted these two weekly sessions, which included instruction in finger painting, Christmas decorations and other arts and crafts. Guests looked forward eagerly to the workshops and took justifiable pride in their accomplishments.

VOLUNTEERS

The new infirmary also had a crop of enthusiastic, youthful volunteers - the candystripers. These senior high school girls from the children's family here responded to a request from Edna G. Boger, R.N., the supervising nurse, for volunteers to assist the registered and practical nurses. The candystripers helped

to take the guests to the dining room, delivered trays to bed-patients, read to guests, answered correspondence and performed many other tasks that brought an added ray of sunshine into the lives of these elderly men and women.

AUXILIARY

Another volunteer group formed that year brought a host of dedicated women into our program of care. The Board of Trustees approved the proposal of Rev. Raymond Heckman and the Public Relations committee to establish a Women's Auxiliary, for the purpose of "expanding the program of activities of our Home family."

In a few months, more than 500 women had enrolled in the auxiliary and plans were underway for their participation. Mrs. Campbell Moatz of Topton was elected as the first President and a goal of 3,000 members was set.

The Women's Auxiliary was contributing to many phases of the program of care. Parties, visits to the bedfast and gifts for the various units were just part of their efforts to serve. At the end of its first year, the Women's Auxiliary boasted 2,561 members, who had provided almost 4,000 volunteer hours of service.

The Lutheran Home noted the passing of Ida L. Henry in March 1964 at the age of 86. Mrs. Henry had been the matron during the years that her late husband, Rev. Jonas O. Henry, was Superintendent.

EDUCATION

Through the years the Trustees, Superintendent and houseparents had emphasized the importance of education. The children were always encouraged to seek higher education, which The Lutheran Home was willing to underwrite. It was most gratifying, therefore, to welcome back Richard L. Gross, who was awarded a bachelor's degree by the Pennsylvania State University as a major in agricultural-biological sciences in mid-year 1963. The young man had spent 10 formative years at the Home and his college education was made possible by the Education and Alumni funds.

The following Spring, a Lutheran Home alumnus, Victor

C. Peischl, was ordained a minister upon graduation from the Lutheran Theological Seminary. He thereby became the sixth "son" to enter the ministry. That year Rev. Reinert

noted in his annual report that the children's family totaled 71 youngsters and there were 123 elderly guests.

A landmark, which would be recalled fondly by many, passed into oblivion when the open air pavilion was razed upon advice by contractors and the architect. Henceforth, a large tent would be rented for Anniversary Day.

In 1966, both the Caum-Unangst and the Henry infirmaries were accredited by the committee on Extended Care Facilities of the American Hospital Association.

This accreditation was a tribute to the dedication and efforts of the Board of Trustees and staff to assure the finest care for the patients in both units.

By that summer, 17 elderly persons were living in the cottage and apartment units which had been built as part of the "cottage plan." Three more cottages were under construction.

HENRY INFIRMARY ADDITION

Early in 1967, construction of the 58 bed addition to the Henry Infirmary got underway. Cost of this project was $804,000 and completion was scheduled for February 1968.

The long-awaited additional beds, increasing the Henry capacity to 98 patients, would enable The Lutheran Home to admit a number of applicants from the ever-lengthening waiting list. The extended care programs had also been certified for Medicare.

In 1967, members of the Women's Auxiliary, whose contribution of 9,649 hours was an amazing record, pledged $13,000 to the Henry Infirmary expansion. Candystripers had devoted 6,228 hours during the year to the comfort and happiness of the elderly guests. Mrs. Carlton L. Heckman of Kutztown was the second President of the Auxiliary.

In 1968, Mrs. Cleona Gallagher, Matron of the Caum Memorial of The Lutheran Home, retired after 11 years of dedicated service. Beginning her work as Director of Activities at the Caum Home, Emily C. Knudsen, widow of the late Rev. Gunnar Knudsen, D.D., pastor of Trinity Lutheran Church of Reading, became Mrs. Gallagher's successor as Matron of the Caum Memorial Home.

REINERT RECEIVES D.D. FROM MUHLENBERG

On June 2, 1968, Muhlenberg College conferred an honorary degree of Doctor of Divinity upon Rev. Webster K. Reinert. As Superintendent of The Lutheran Home for 22 years, Dr. Reinert had demonstrated remarkable administrative abilities. Even more important was his vision of the future role of the Home in an era of changing needs and new patterns of care. He and his wife, Mary, were making a monumental contribution to this program.

At the 71st Anniversary Day, August 10, 1968, the highlight was the dedication of the biggest single project to date - the addition to the Henry Infirmary. The Lutheran Home was again dramatically expanding its program of care to the aged by adding accommodations for 58 more guests. The Henry addition was the last word in modern care facilities.

The growing family of aged guests dictated the addition of a full-time Director of Activities to develop group activity programs. Mrs. Wilbur Herring was named to this post and immediately began an effective schedule of events that would enrich the lives of the elderly.

Under her direction the publication of a monthly campus newspaper, G'Schichta, which means "happenings" in Pennsylvania German, made its appearance.

Early in the same year, the need for giving guidance and direction to a growing number of volunteers indicated the importance of naming a Director of Volunteer Services. Mrs. Campbell Moatz of Topton was added to the staff of the Home on a part-time basis to direct the volunteer program.

That summer the death of 80-year old Clair Carl was noted as another indication of the many decades of care provided by the Lutheran Home. Mr. Carl and his sister, Sallie, were the first orphans to be admitted 71 years earlier.

The Women's Auxiliary continued its good works and the Board of Trustees expressed their gratitude for a gift of $13,000 from the indefatigable ladies, which was earmarked for the construction and furnishing of two craft rooms.

NEW CHILDREN'S PROGRAM

A plan to intensify the children's program was approved by the Trustees early in 1969. The committee headed by Rev. Paul J. Henry recommended the addition of more boys and girls between the ages of 10 and 18 who could not easily be placed in foster homes. It was estimated that the plan would cost $100,000 for up to 30 such children. The committee's report was based upon current referrals and the needs expressed by local children's agencies. It was a bold step into a new phase of care.

Everyone mourned the death of Rev. Raymond J. Heckman, D.D., of Allentown in Feb. 1968. He had been Vice-President of the Board of Trustees. Rev. Frank E. Radcliffe, D.D., was selected to fill his unexpired term.

Rev. Reinert reported that 52 children had been served by The Lutheran Home during 1968, with 36 listed as guests at the end of that year. A decision was made to employ a full-time Director of Children's Services, as an important step in a new approach demanded by changing times and attitudes.

The venerable old Main Building, which had housed so many hundreds of children over seven decades, would perform this function no more. The Superintendent announced that, henceforth, all resident children would live in the Allentown Conference Cottage for Boys, the Memorial Cottage for Senior Boys and the Kehl-Charles Memorial for Girls. Rev. Reinert noted, "We are rapidly approaching the time when we must make a decision as to the future use of the Main Building."

A total of 159 elderly men and women were guests at the end of 1968. The cottage-apartment plan, now in its eighth year, continued to grow and Luther Haven's 27 units were "home" to 47 people.

Updating of the children's program continued. More than $28,000 was spent on renovations and improvements to the children's cottages during 1969.

And what a job the volunteers were doing! At the end of the year, Mrs. Campbell Moatz, Director of Volunteers, reported that 52,272 hours of service had been provided by candystripers and individual and group volunteers since the program's inception in 1963. The Women's Auxiliary had established a gift shop in the Henry Infirmary to serve visitors, patients and staff.

On December 30, 1963, Richard T. Williamson, the President of the Board of Trustees, died at the age of 59. Atty. Williamson had been President for 18 years. His service as Solicitor and Trustee dated back to 1948. Dick Williamson was always "a man who stood straight and tall among us." He left an indelible mark upon the institution to which he devoted so much of his time and abundant talents.

A few weeks later, Charles K. Emhardt, a member of the Board for almost 18 years, died unexpectedly at age 73.

"In view of the growing waiting list of the aged awaiting admission, the Board of Trustees approved tentative plans for the placement of 16 additional beds in the new wing of the Henry Infirmary."

This terse announcement in <u>The Herald</u> of Winter 1970 was evidence of the unflagging efforts of the Trustees to meet the ever-increasing need for facilities for the aged.

The Superintendent announced that The Lutheran Home, in 1969, had given $159,941 in free service to children and aging guests. This sum was the difference between the ability of some guests to pay and the cost of their care for the year.

In July 1969, The Lutheran Home organized a Social Services Department and the purchase of case work service through the Lutheran Children's Bureau was discontinued. Miss Getha Bomboy, M.S., ACSW, supervised the social work staff.

Rev. Frank Radcliffe, D.D., was elected President of the Board and J. Park Smith of Topton was named Treasurer to replace Harold C. Aulenbach who had resigned. Two new Board members were welcomed - Rev. Charles M. Kern of Allentown and Lawrence J. Reimert, Ph.D., of Schnecksville in Lehigh County.

Approval of a record $1,377,000 budget for 1971 dramatically demonstrated the expanding program of the Home. This budget anticipated a deficit of $235,000 in the budget for the year. William E. Yoder of Kutztown was elected to the Board of Trustees.

In a few short years, 74 beds had been added to the Henry Infirmary. Now the Trustees made plans for an East Wing to the building, which would house still more beds for the elderly who awaited admission.

It was in 1971 that Mary E. Belser concluded a long and dedicated career at The Lutheran Home. Miss Belser came to Topton in 1926 as a teacher in the school, a position she filled for 20 years. Then she accepted the post of office secretary and receptionist, which she held until her retirement. An integral part of The Lutheran Home for almost a half-century, Mary Belser announced that she would continue to perform full-time volunteer services.

In April Rev. Rufus E. Kern, D.D., the Luther Haven pioneer and Board member for a dozen years, died at age of 84. Luther Haven now had 73 residents.

That Spring, Rev. Webster K. Reinert and his wife celebrated their silver anniversary as Superintendent and

Matron of the Home. During their tenure, the program of care was altered and expanded to meet the changing needs of children and the elderly. Through his dedicated and inspired service, Dr. Reinert played a key role in this unceasing effort.

In his annual report to the Corporation, the Superintendent announced that 181 elderly guests and 40 children were included in The Lutheran Home's family. The Board of Trustees was increased from 18 to 24; 12 clergy and 12 lay directors. Rev. Elton P. Richards, Jr., of Reading was elected and soon three women were to become Directors - Mrs. Arline Trexler, Allentown; Dr. Dorothea Kleppinger, Reading, and Emalyn R. Weiss, Wyomissing.

In the Summer of 1971, The Lutheran Home launched a new Foster Care Program. The program was designed to aid children to find new families, where they could be a part of a normal home with parents who could give them individual help and attention. Seven boys and girls were placed in foster homes immediately though this plan. By the end of the year, the Women's Auxiliary boasted 3,725 members, whose contributions to the program of care continued to amaze the trustees and staff. Mrs. Paul Carlson of Kutztown was the third President of the Auxiliary.

The Lutheran Home was also reaching out into the community in its efforts to serve the elderly confined to their homes. Meals on Wheels was launched late in 1971 and 14 persons were being served their daily meals in their homes by a group of 40 volunteers. The meals were prepared in the kitchen. This program is now contractual.

The Lutheran Home suffered a severe loss in August of 1971 when Harold C. Barette of Allentown died suddenly. Mr. Barette, a member of the Board of Trustees for 13 years, had performed dedicated service.

Plans were being made for renovation of the former George E. Holton Memorial Cottage for Infants. This fourth children's unit on the Topton campus would serve as an emergency placement center.

The staff had grown to 190 persons and the need for a

Director of Personnel was becoming more apparent. As 1971 came to a close, the Trustees were seeking a professional person to fill this role and also act as administrative assistant to Rev. Reinert.

During that year, 87 children had been served, and the family of 47 youngsters on December 31 included eight Blacks and three Puerto Ricans. There were 205 elderly guests and 77 people were residing in Luther Haven as part of the plan for individual retirement living.

As The Lutheran Home at Topton approached its 75th birthday in 1972, the Trustees, staff and growing army of volunteers could reflect with pride on the ever-increasing accomplishments of this institution that was dedicated to "providing for them."

This three-quarters of a century of Christian service to the homeless that began in 1896 had never ceased to embody the prophetic words, "We deem it advisable to take steps toward providing for the homeless orphans and half orphans of our congregations."

The writer of that report could not have predicted the problems of the aging that would one day make The Lutheran Home a two-phase program of care.

Over the years they came - the orphans, the children from broken homes, aged individuals and, later, couples who would spend their golden years in the cottages and apartments. The hand of welcome was always outstretched and the Trustees, Superintendent and staff sought new and better ways to make life here happy and meaningful.

The rewards for Rev. & Mrs. Reinert were modest by worldly standards. But their treasures were those that can only be piled up by unselfish service, tireless dedication and an abiding compassion for the homeless. This is the example that The Lutheran Home at Topton will always be to a troubled world.

Chapter 8

NEW DIRECTIONS

The Rev. Paul L. Buehrle, D.D. 1975-1995

Rev. Buehrle's eyes twinkled as he recalled being considered to lead The Lutheran Home. "Don't tell anyone, but I was so excited about this opportunity that I would have taken it for no salary! I'd never been to the Topton campus, but I surely knew of its reputation. The offer was a dream come true."

He was born and grew up in Bucks County in a little community called Blooming Glen. He was a graduate of Muhlenberg College (Allentown) and the Lutheran Theological Seminary (Philadelphia.) After graduation, he served parishes in Weissport, PA and Milford and Wilmington, DE, prior to becoming the Executive Director of the Wilmington Senior Center, Inc., Wilmington, DE. His considerable experience delivering social services to the community and through the Church made him a

The Rev. Paul L. Buehrle, D.D.
President

prime candidate for the Lutheran Home position.

He recalls, "Jim Rahn, CEO at Tressler Lutheran Services, was consulting with The Lutheran Home at Topton. Tressler was operating in Delaware, so he knew what was happening." He asked Paul Buehrle if he would be willing to talk with the search committee.

The search committee DID talk to him (among others) and the offer was made. "I was very enthused, because this is exactly what I wanted to do," he grinned.

On May 21, 1975, the Board of Trustees of The Lutheran Home at Topton announced the appointment of Rev. Paul L. Buehrle of Wilmington, Delaware as the new President/ CEO of The Lutheran Home at Topton and its Reading Campus, Caum Memorial Home. Pastor Buehrle assumed his new duties in August of 1975.

From the beginning, the top job had been a 'team effort,' made up of a husband-and-wife team; the Superintendent and Matron. This was particularly appropriate when the prime mission was the operation of an orphanage. But times were changing. In the previous administration, Rev. Reinert correctly identified his term as "the transition." It was now time for a different type of leader, much more of an administrative director.

Paul and his wife, Betty, moved from Wilmington and settled into the President's Home. "It was a good thing to see what was going on. It was an excellent way to get to know the staff."

'THE WAY IT WAS'

He recalls 'the way it was' when he arrived:

· "We still had 92 beds for children on the campus. The kids were not the same type as in years past; some were really difficult! The Luther Haven residents were full of apprehension; the conflict between this type of child and retired adults was a strain. Pennsylvania was pushing to de-institutionalize children. They felt the children should be in the 'least restrictive setting.' We started to phase out the beds on campus. When the phaseout was completed, we were left with six vacant buildings."

· Pastor Buehrle was given a mandate to make certain that, in addition to the residential services for children and the older adults, ministries would be provided for the larger community. This is one of the most dramatic changes in the mission; more on this later.

· The need to provide more care and services for the elderly, identified by Rev. John Raker over 90 years before, was now becoming more and more urgent. Bear in mind that this planning, under Rev. Buehrle's direction, was FAR in advance of the public's new awareness of the present "aging baby-boomer" generation.

· It's all very well to have great plans for the elderly and the larger community. What was staring him in the face was 92 vacant beds in six buildings. He was charged with the responsibility of making certain that the 97-bed Intermediate Health Care Unit that was under construction on the campus be occupied.

CHANGES AT CAUM MEMORIAL HOME

If THOSE problems weren't enough, another one appeared in Reading. The Lutheran Home had requested permission to build an addition to the Caum Memorial Home at 1711 Hampden Boulevard.

The need for an addition to the Caum Memorial Home was prompted by the merger of the Home for Widows and Single Women in Reading and The Lutheran Home organization.

The Home for Widows and Single Women building was going to be abandoned and those residents would be moving either to the Topton campus or to the Caum Memorial building in Reading.

The addition requested was denied because of objections by local community residents, neighbors to Caum Memorial. (Obviously, the NIMBY phenomenon..."Not In MY Back Yard" was happening then.)

Note here, once again, how Topton's leadership team steps back, regroups, recycles and re-invents its identity.

The program had to be changed immediately. The merger was effected, the sale of the former Home for Widows and Single Women was finalized. Caum Memorial Home was converted to a personal care facility. All skilled nursing beds from Caum would be moved to the Topton campus. *As you might imagine, all of the above took a lot more doing than is contained in these few lines of type. This was certainly a major program.*

Here's a first-hand look from Dorthie Kaylor, now Admissions Coordinator, at what these changes meant:

"When Rev. Buehrle and Kathy Wilson said they would phase out Caum, we knew the patients would be transferred to Topton. The only ones to stay would be strictly residential. We met with Dr. Gable, our Medical Director, to get word on who would be asked to come to Topton.

"Rev. Buehrle and Mrs. Wilson suggested that I would take over as Acting Director of Nursing. They needed someone to direct and give them guidance on the new ICF unit. I got a little office in the back.

"Sharon Leiby, a nurses' aide, was my right arm. I said, 'We need some organization, guidance and direction. You need to hire people if you expect to fill the beds and bring all my people from Caum.'

"Transferring took weeks; ambulance arrangements were complicated, and that was just to move the residents. Thank goodness for volunteers and families who had to bring up all their clothing and furniture.

"Dr. Gable and I tried to put the Caum patients where they would be best suited, so they would have the best trained nurses.

"Florence Newcomer was a resident at Caum for many years and was transferred. She had a beautiful grandfather's clock. We placed it in the Fireplace Lounge. It was a gift. Florence said: 'I want it with me. When I die, it stays right where it is!'

"We had to build our own nurses' units within each of the seven units, with supervisors, charge nurses and staff nurses on each. One person took care of medications...she just 'flew' around!

"I knew we needed a better way to manage. We were understaffed. I had to have nurses on 'per diem' until we could hire full-timers. Thank goodness for the five-year nursing program at Albright College. They helped a lot. Some students worked 3-11 or 11-7 to help us out.

"I looked for nurses who liked elderly people. Where could you find a better group than the ones from Fleetwood, Blandon, Bowers and Kutztown? In that era, grandparents were still living at home. I was looking for that kind of background, in addition to enough experience."

WHAT'S GOING ON?

Over the years, it's been hard for the public to understand 'what's going on at The Lutheran Home at Topton.' First, its location is away from the population centers of Reading, Allentown and Pottsville. Second, except for the staff, Board and some visitors, primarily on Anniversary Day, few came to call. Third: even if you came, you'd need a tour and explanation to learn about the specialized services.

Result: people developed an 'understanding' of what it was...usually incomplete and years out of date. And, because the reputation had been excellent, there was no need to spend any more time on it. This presented a continuing dilemma: how do we get the word out? It's expensive, it SEEMS self-serving, and it's always changing.

How to get the word out? Every possible way! The first communications tool was <u>The Orphans' Paper</u>. It became <u>The Herald</u>, which has changed over the years from a small glossy newsletter to its present large tabloid format. There are now brochures and literature for most of the divisions; audio and videotapes, etc. The attitude now is that the changing story MUST get out. It is vital to the mission.

The Lutheran Home organization was starting to show real growth. The Board agreed to hire its first full-time Chaplain, Rev. Charles Kern. This allowed Pastor Buehrle to devote his full time to administration.

Pastor Buehrle and Chaplain Charles Kern were installed into their new positions of responsibility on February 17, 1976. During that same service of installation, there was also a service of dedication for the new 97 bed intermediate care addition to the Henry Health Care Center.

Remember the 97 beds? By April 1976, all Caum Memorial intermediate care patients had been transferred to the Topton campus.

Earlier in the chapter, we referred to Pastor Buehrle's mission to provide more community service. **Every change is either a challenge or a problem**. Changes of all kinds were happening simultaneously. Watch how Pastor Buehrle and his team handled THIS one. It's fascinating!

Pastor Buehrle's pattern has been:

> . identify the need

> . define the program

> . hire the best person

FAMILY LIFE SERVICES

Rev. Conrad W. Weiser, Ph.D. was the first director of Family Life Services (FLS) in 1977. We spoke with Terry A. Lieb, FLS Director since 1980. Lieb thinks back: "I worked at Bethany Children's Home (UCC.) I knew The Lutheran Home at Topton had been an orphanage. When I came here in April of 1980, I felt I'd been given a lifetime opportunity to integrate my faith in my work. It was a major turning point; I gave up a dream home, security and structure.

"I've been given freedom and support and ability to cause change; this is most valuable to me. Pastor Buehrle is affirming, supportive of our programs. He says: 'Be creative' and:

> . don't lose sight of your goals

> . don't make decisions on profits or money

> . mission goals are the basis for decisions

"The Lutheran Home has not forced any programs. They honor our goals. For instance, we charge based on ability to

Terry A. Lieb
Director, Family Life
Services

pay. Some of our competitors increased their fees to $50/hour. They are now gone. We listen to the changing needs. Sure, we're going through hard budget times. We have to be flexible.

"Families today are at risk. Typically, our clients are divorced. The traditional family is at risk. What's lacking? Intimacy, time together, a sense of security. We do a lot in churches; conflict and crisis resolution. I feel we need to do more prevention work.

Jim Giamotti, FLS

"The growth of our programs has been simultaneous with great personal growth. This is so much different than the state system. I can see it every day.

"In a way, it's frightening, because I could never go back to my old job again. This is too exciting here."

By publication date, Family Life Services has grown to provide these services on an annual basis:

1,207 Counseled

39 Couples in Pre-marriage Series

18 Pastoral Care teams trained

2,000 in Employee Assistance Program

526 in drug/alcohol related programming

  86 families in drug intervention assessment

3,876 clients served

To recap: The Lutheran Home's missions were serving children and now the elderly. Another significant activity was "bubbling up." This would shortly result in a third division of service for The Lutheran Home at Topton: **The Family Life Services Division**. The program developed out of an expressed interest of The Lutheran Churches in the Schuylkill Mission district. Those congregations wanted some social ministry delivery for their area.

They requested that we give serious consideration to developing a program that would serve their members. A committee was put together represented by The Lutheran Home at Topton, the Northeastern Synod and the Inner Mission Society of Berks and Schuylkill, East Berks and West Berks Mission Districts.

The result of that committee activity was a program known as Family Life Services. That program began in 1977 and continues to the present. Family Life Services provides counseling and support services to individuals and families in need. The individual counseling is provided by an extended staff of professional counselors who are at the masters and/or doctoral level of expertise and are available in various sections of the Synod. In order to make travel distance less painful for the clients, they meet in local churches or other community settings throughout Berks and Schuylkill Counties in order to provide and assist the client with the kind of professional counsel and expertise that helps them through their crisis.

In addition to professional counseling, the program also provides workshops and support groups throughout the service area. These services address a variety of issues, i.e.:

loss of spouse, suicide, unemployment, congregational crises and clergy assistance.

Pastors are provided free consultations by FLS professionals as they seek support and assistance in their own counseling situations within their parish.

EMPLOYMENT COUNSELING AND CONSULTATION SERVICE

A more recent addition to the Family Life Service delivery system is an Employee Assistance Program. Employers throughout the territory engage our Family Life Services Department to provide counseling services for their employees whenever those employees are in particular kinds of crises or difficulty that might hamper or hinder their effectiveness in the workplace. An extremely effective and helpful service for our Lutheran congregations is the program known as Pastoral Care teams.

PASTORAL CARE

Pastoral Care, another FLS service, assists in spreading out the counseling load of pastors in local congregations. FLS trains persons within the congregation to be support counselors for the pastor to help assist others through times of trouble and crisis. The Family Life Services Department enables The Lutheran Home to really expand its community ministry outreach into all of the corners of the Synod in a way that is both meaningful and beneficial to the Church. It is also helpful to the members of the Pastoral Care teams. Theirs is the joy of giving of one's own self.

NEW SYNODS FORMED

In October, 1968, the Eastern Pennsylvania Synod of the Lutheran Church in America divided into the Southeastern and Northeastern Synods. The Lutheran Children and Family Services program had its home office in Philadelphia and branch offices in Reading, Bethlehem and Pottsville.

The Lutheran Home at Topton was the social ministry agency of the Northeastern Pennsylvania Synod responsible for delivering children's services to the entire Synod. Thus, they were asked to manage the portion of the program in the NEPA Synod. The Lutheran Home was more than willing to be of service in this fashion. The Lutheran Home at Topton inherited the existing branch offices in Reading, Bethlehem and Pottsville.

In addition, the new Synod program transfer included a home for single mothers located in Bethlehem. This home for single mothers operated as a treatment program, starting during pregnancy. After the girls had their babies, they stayed at a planned location, so their child could be cared for while they went to school or to work. The program then assisted the girl to make a decision whether she would raise the child or give her child up for adoption. The necessary counseling was handled by the casework department of The Lutheran Home at Topton.

At the time of this transfer, there were 92 beds on the Topton campus for children, including elementary school age to teenagers. There were four cottages for boys, a girl's cottage and a cottage to house a Diagnostic Unit program for boys in need of serious rehabilitation.

The Lutheran Home was now well established as a comprehensive organization for services for children AND older adults. In 1976, The Lutheran Home had over 250 children and over 350 older adults in its care.

SERVICES TO CHILDREN

This multi-faceted treatment program serves children up to 18 years of age. Designed to be a rehabilitative treatment process, the program is set up to enable the child to plan to eventually return to its natural family.

Program categories have included the following:

Adoption - places infants, children with special needs, and hard-to-place children in homes of persons seeking to adopt a child. The Home has reciprocal agreements with adoption exchanges both in the United States and overseas.

Institutional Treatment - a cottage that housed 14 boys was located on the Topton campus to provide treatment for boys requiring intensive, therapeutic care.

Community Living Centers - a network of living facilities that ranged from group homes to a transistory program for children ready to leave institutional care. These professional foster homes were family structured and were located in a variety of urban, suburban, and rural settings. The maximum capacity of these homes was three children.

Foster Family Care - a treatment mode of temporary parental care for children who must leave their natural families. Children from infancy to 18 years of age are helped to recover permanency either by returning to their natural home, being adopted, or being placed in long-term foster care. A unique part of this program is specialized care for children with special needs such as blindness, Down's Syndrome, terminal illness, emotional problems, etc.

Orientation House - a unique residential program for boys aged 13 to 18 was located at 1145 Walnut Street in Allentown. It was a transitional placement for either pre- or post- institutional care. The program offered a treatment mode based on a systematic human relation training model.

Problem Pregnancy - offers a special service to young women who become pregnant outside of marriage, as well as for married persons for whom pregnancy creates a physical, emotional, or financial problem.

Counseling - a cooperative program with the Allentown Area Lutheran Parish to serve problem children and their families in dealing with the issues of life.

RISE AND FALL OF ORPHANAGES

In the late 19th century, orphanages were hailed as "ideal institutions." In comparison to what else was available, this had been true. And, in those days, life was pretty insular and self-contained. It was difficult to find people who had been out of their state or region. By the mid-20th century, the United States had become the leading industrialized nation in the world, fought two world wars and was much more a nation with an ever-stronger national government.

There was a GREAT DEAL more government. Regulatory agencies controlled a lot more of our lives. The "new thinking" in child care was swinging to foster or group home care. It was felt that a "family atmosphere" was much more desirable for children than being "institutionalized." It didn't matter that The Lutheran Home at Topton had been one of the best orphanages. It was now a dinosaur.

The Pennsylvania legislature passed regulations that required that children be de-institutionalized. The hope was that the children should have the privilege and opportunity to grow up in a more familiar household setting with a family type atmosphere. Hopefully, they would also have that family atmosphere once they went back to their own families.

The children housed on the Topton campus were relocated into group homes in the community, supervised by houseparents. Children assigned to foster families were added to the existing family to gain experiences of a family setting. Six buildings on the Topton campus, which formerly housed orphans, were now vacant. However, the adoption programs continued. Adoptions were both national and international in scope.

This was a time of great change which would alter all of the programs of The Lutheran Home at Topton. This challenge would provide the opportunity to add additional programs, which would make the organization one of the leading social ministry delivery organizations in the entire Northeastern Pennsylvania corridor.

GOVERNMENT REGULATIONS ...AND MEALTIME

The government was "the man who came to dinner." As reimbursement dollars for children and older adults were received, so were the regulations that applied to these clients. One such state inspection mandated separate menus for children and for aging residents.

What did that MEAN? The Lutheran Home had to redesign its kitchen, menus and meal delivery. And that meant MONEY. So the Women's Auxiliary of The Lutheran Home at Topton came to the rescue again! They agreed to share the burden of this cost so that the kitchen could be designed to meet these regulatory requirements.

The Auxiliary, which began in 1963, had grown to well over 4,000 members. They were very instrumental in raising funds for necessary projects so The Lutheran Home at Topton could continue to deliver first-rate services for those looking to it for support and meaningful existence.

CHURCH COUNCILS

As you might expect, changes like this do not come easily, nor do they come without stress, pain and consternation. In addition, the financial cost was staggering. In order to try to relieve some of that pressure, the Board of Trustees approved the position of Director of Development.

This director was to begin a very comprehensive activity of fundraising to support the programs of The Lutheran Home at Topton and to help with all of these adjustments. One such creative program: church councils were invited to have their council meeting on the Topton campus.

They were provided a nice dinner, then given a brief report and video about The Lutheran Home at Topton. This helped many congregational church councils to have a better appreciation and understanding for the ministries of The Lutheran Home at Topton.

We've talked several times about the way The Lutheran Home constantly reinvents and recreates itself. Here's a perfect example. The state mandates the end of orphanages, leaving us with several empty buildings. *Now what?*

RECYCLING BUILDINGS

One of the children's buildings was changed into a day care center for employees' youngsters who needed a place to stay during the day while their parents worked. Another building was converted into offices for the children's department. A third building that was a recent gift (the Koch-

Knauss Memorial Cottage) was converted into housing for older adults. The three remaining buildings were razed to make room for an apartment complex; a continuing care retirement community for older adults.

As the years of the orphanage drew to a close, many complained about the passing of an age. What they did **not** see were the huge new opportunities which were coming! It enabled a major expansion of services to older adults.

That expansion took place in a number of ways on the Topton campus; in new locations out in the community and in changes of program and service delivery to older adults all over Northeastern Pennsylvania. It began with a day care program at Caum Memorial in Reading in 1977 that was a partnership arrangement with the Berks County Agency on Aging and continued through all the expansion listed here.

The medical delivery system was enhanced with the addition of three new staff physicians, all of whom became nationally certified geriatricians.

SERVING THE AGING

Quality of service and caring attitude in which it is delivered is the prime concern of those entrusted with providing care to retired residents living in facilities on all The Lutheran Home's campuses. A wide variety of social, recreational, spiritual, and support services are available to meet the needs of residents from independent living to total nursing care.

CONTINUING CARE RETIREMENT COMMUNITIES

In 1995, continuing care facilities are no longer front-page news. Many congregations now have them; private corporations put them up. The entire U.S. economy is finally aware of the huge potential market in 'aging baby-boomers'. However, going back over two decades, few comprehended the need. Fewer had the 'intestinal fortitude' to take the risk and make it happen.

Another round of applause for the Board of Directors, the President and management team. Once again, The Lutheran Home was on the 'cutting edge!'

Pastor Buehrle recalls: "We were planning to build all the retirement community structures here. The feasibility study indicated that there would be more interest in the Allentown area rather than Topton."

Luther Crest Retirement Community

LUTHER CREST

The Board of Trustees approved the building of "continuing care retirement communities." The site for the Luther Crest complex was approved by the Board of Trustees following the activity of a small committee that looked at five separate possible sites in the Lehigh Valley area. The selected site is within easy access to Route I-78, Route 22, Route 309, and Tilghman Street, all major arteries.

Luther Crest was built in suburban Allentown. The complex contains 310 apartment units, all interconnected to a central portion of the building that included dining, medical care, dental care, podiatry care, ophthalmogy care in the medical suite, plus 60 nursing beds.

It includes a library, recreation rooms and activity rooms, along with a multi-purpose room in the center of the community section called Crest Hall. In addition, there are administrative offices. Luther Crest was designed, along with Tower Court, as a complex that would guarantee care for as long as a person lives.

Luther Crest was opened in 1983, and in 1991, a personal care wing was added that provided 29 additional beds with a level of service that included in-service training, volunteer service and additional activity facilities.

Tower Court Retirement Community

TOWER COURT

Tower Court was built on the Topton campus. The Tower Court facility comprises 50 apartment units which were attached to the existing Henry Health Care facility of 229 nursing beds on one end, and to the Old Main building on the other. They offer an independent lifestyle, free from household and maintenance worries with meal service, linen, housekeeping and transportation services. Tower Court offers junior one bedroom, one bedroom and two bedroom apartments. Each apartment is equipped with an emergency call bell system should the need for help arise.

CAUM MEMORIAL HOME

Located at 1711 Hampden Boulevard, Reading, Caum provides a beautiful residence for 33 retired persons. This personal care facility offers each resident the tranquility of a private room, yet the social opportunities of communal living.

From left: Lillian Gougler, Theodora Hildesbrand and Alice McCord enjoy a Hallowee'n Party at the Caum Memorial Home.

Luther Haven Neighborhood

LUTHER HAVEN

A residential community on the Topton campus includes 54 cottages plus five Koch-Knauss apartments, the Krum Cottage and the Forrest Cottage. While these residences offer complete independence, residents actively participate in various programs and activities, including volunteer service.

Luther Meadows

LUTHER MEADOWS & HEILMAN HOUSE

In addition to Tower Court and Luther Crest, The Lutheran Home applied for and received funding for a rent-subsidized retirement living apartment house which would house 50 apartments and come to be known as Luther Meadows. Built on the Topton campus, it was dedicated in 1982 and provided services for those on limited incomes. Residents are invited to participate actively in all programs of The Lutheran Home, as well as their own Senior Citizens Club which meets weekly. Heilman House added an additional 50 units of housing for limited-income residents.

Heilman House

The rent subsidy provided by the federal government made possible a partnership with the government to provide housing for people who need this kind of care. To make room for new buildings, it was necessary to take down all the farm buildings except for the farmhouse (the original orphans' home.) While change is always a challenge, it is the only constant. The times had changed; the mission had changed and expanded. The response was 'on target.'

When Heilman House was completed in 1990, The Lutheran Home had 100 apartments for low-income elderly as well as physically challenged adults over the age of 18. Heilman House was named after the first Superintendent of The Lutheran Home at Topton. Two additional cottages were built in our Luther Haven development. There were now 55 cottages on the Topton campus.

THE HIGHLANDS AT WYOMISSING

In addition to those facilities, The Lutheran Home entered into a joint venture with the Reading Hospital and built The Highlands at Wyomissing. The complex has 275 apartments, 30 personal care beds and 60 skilled nursing beds.

Dr. Bob Boyer polishes the front door while Don Griffith 'considers' buffing the roof.

Dedicated in 1989, it stands as a landmark in cooperative ministry with another well-respected community service organization, the Reading Hospital.

LUTHER RIDGE

While all of these projects were under way, a personal care facility was being constructed in Pottsville, PA. It had 84

Luther Ridge

beds and was named Luther Ridge. This personal care complex allowed the servicing of Schuylkill County clientele. Luther Ridge was dedicated in 1990.

After discussing all of the residential services, Pastor Buehrle stopped and grinned. "We keep learning, because things keep changing.

The demographics are fascinating. In 1983, the average 'move-in' age was 74.4. In 1990, it was up to 81. People are moving in later. They are living longer. Even more interesting, they are staying healthy longer. We now have vacant apartments; we will convert some to assisted living. We'll ALWAYS need a marketing department!"

229	Henry Health Care Center
33	Caum Home
60	Luther Crest Health Care
29	Luther Crest Personal Care
449	Luther Crest Apartments
71	Luther Meadows
72	Heilman House
72	Tower Court Apartments
105	Luther Ridge
7	Koch-Knauss Apartments
104	Luther Haven
602	The Highlands
1,833	residents served

Resident Activities - Every facility operated by The Lutheran Home offers a range of organized activities designed to meet the individual and collective needs of the residents. Under the guidance of an activities director with assistants (a staff of three at Luther Crest and five at The Lutheran Home), each facility provides regularly scheduled events as well as special events. Exercise classes, arts and crafts sessions, and sing-alongs are held daily or weekly, while birthday parties are held monthly.

Each residence has activities which distinguish it from the others. For example, at the Caum Home, residents attend outdoor concerts at Gring's Mill. Residents of Luther Crest are involved in the activities of the community.

Space was given to a local church organizing a Sunday school class for handicapped youngsters. Residents hosted a Chamber of Commerce mixer and decorated and contributed a Christmas tree to the Festival of Trees sponsored by the Auxiliary to the Lehigh County Medical Society.

Day trips and excursions are an important part of the calendar of events. Residents of the Topton campus, for example, journey to the Poconos for the Fall foliage, lunch and shop at Brickerville House and attend music and cultural events.

Nursing Care - Nursing care residents often need a full range of social and related services for physical, spiritual, and financial support. Their independence, however, is not sacrificed. They choose their daily menu and determine for themselves their degree of participation in activities.

Nursing - Licensed skilled and intermediate care is available round-the-clock at the 229 bed Henry Infirmary on the Topton campus and the 60 bed Luther Crest Health Care Center on the Allentown campus. The nursing staff gives specialized care, such as the administration of medication and personalized assistance in activities for daily living.

Medical - The Lutheran Home has a full-time medical staff of three physicians. Medical Directors, Ward G. Becker, M.D., Raymond J. Hauser, M.D., and Carol A. Slompak, M.D., have been honored by the Reading Hospital and Medical Center as Teachers of the Year for their preceptorship program in conjunction with medical residents in the Family Practice Program during a geriatric rotation at The Lutheran Home.

Physical Therapy - The physical therapy department provides a wide range of rehabilitative therapies to residents and outpatient clients. The department offers the most recent treatments in the areas of orthopedics, neuro-surgical and sports medicine, including electro-acupuncture techniques designed to reduce or eliminate pain.

Pastoral Care - To talk with a resident who feels the need, to pray with a resident in time of joy or sadness, to administer the sacrament of the Lord's Supper in the privacy of their own room - these are some of the daily duties of the department of Pastoral Care.

There was a strengthening of visitations with residents and participation in many of the spiritual programs by the chaplain, a part-time pastor, a shared intern, three clinical pastoral education students and local pastors who volunteered their time on all three campuses.

Bible study at the three campuses complimented the fifth annual "Week of Good News." This week of special religious emphasis was possible because of the excellent efforts from local churches.

All of these services have been aimed at helping older persons live meaningful and satisfying lives in a comfortable and secure environment. Each person is treated with care and dignity, and is encouraged to be independent in every possible way.

SENIOR NEIGHBORHOOD CENTERS

These partnership arrangements, put together with the Area Agency on Aging in Berks County, made it possible to develop Senior Neighborhood Centers that were located in community buildings or in churches.

They provide daily meals and socialization for older adults in ten locations in Robesonia, Birdsboro, Kutztown, Hamburg, Boyertown and Reading. The ten centers are open

Monday through Friday from 9 a.m. to 3 p.m. A noontime meal is served to any person age 60 or older.

Right on the Beat!
(From left:)
Ruth I.Baumener,
Edward A.
Baumener,
Estella
Hamilton

Enjoying the Game!
(from left)
Mary Gehret,
Bertha Nocho

Volunteers at each Senior Center site package individual meals for home delivery.

In addition, Senior Centers presented social/recreational programs, nutrition education programs and tax counseling sessions. The YWCA Camp has hosted "Young At Heart" campers for a week-long, residential camping program. The Wyomissing Foundation provided financial support for this unique experience.

An emphasis on programs and services for Hispanic senior citizens in Reading initiated the opening of the Hispanic Senior Center during 1988. The Lutheran Home hired a bi-lingual communication outreach specialist to facilitate that process.

    510   Case Management Services

    685   Tax Counseling Services

  1,195   clients served

MEALS-ON-WHEELS

Out of the Senior Neighborhood Center programs, The Lutheran Home at Topton also assumed the responsibility for Meals-on-Wheels in both Berks and Schuylkill Counties. Meals are provided for those older adults who are unable to leave their home or who can't function properly within their own home.

These meals are delivered by volunteers who make it possible for those confined to their home to have some contact with the outside world, as well as to receive the necessary dietary supplements required for good health. (It's not just the food, it's the contact with people who smile and talk to you!)

371	clients in Berks County
<u>550</u>	clients in Schuylkill County
921	clients served

George Ferrero
Highlands Staff Volunteer

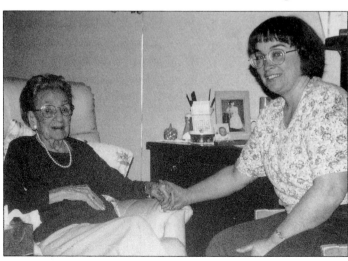

From left: Effie Schlenker, Nancy Plushanski

VOLUNTEER HOME CARE

Another expansion of program services included the development of a home health program to help people stay in their own homes longer. Added to this Medicare approved program was a Volunteer Home Care Program that provides support services for people in their own homes, i.e.: writing letters, caring for the house, doing the laundry, mowing the lawn, running errands, helping to fix small repairs around the property, etc.

275 clients in Schuylkill County

<u>240</u> clients in Berks County

515 clients served

LATINO SOCIAL SERVICES/INNER MISSION

In response to the pressing need for social work services among Latinos in Reading, The Lutheran Home began to hire bilingual staff. An intergenerational breakfast program was begun in two locations. This was continued until the Reading School District began to offer its own breakfast program. Social workers were employed to assist the pastors of the Lutheran congregation offering worship in Spanish with the needs of the growing Latino population.

With the projection that, by the year 2000, the Latino population may be half the population in Reading, this work continues to expand, including an after-school club for children, tutoring by college students in several elementary schools, teenage pregnancy support groups and counseling, plus a growing case load of both adults and children.

Over many years, the Lutheran Inner Mission Society of Berks and Schuylkill and The Lutheran Home at Topton had shared in serving the same primary territory. Conversations about merger had taken place from time to time. The Bishop of the Northeastern Pennsylvania Synod

A Gift of Love

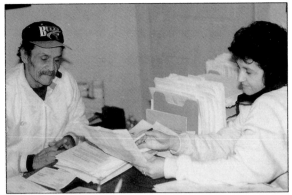

named a committee representing the two agencies and the three districts and charged them with developing a plan which led to a merger that took effect on January 1, 1992.

Juan Torrez
& Ruby Lenovich

Feliz Navidad!
Packing up presents are
(from left)
Ruth Santiago,
Ruby Alba-Lenovich,
Marcolina Morales

1,600	Lutheran Pantry
198	Case-load adults
685	Senior Neighbor-hood Centers
2,483	clients served

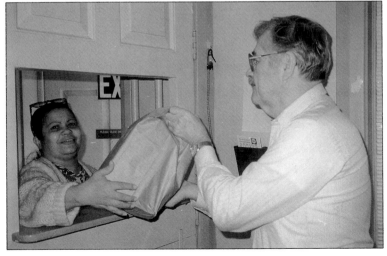

John Biel,
Lutheran
Pantry

Pearl Brady, Inner Mission Com. Min. & Rev. Paul Schaediger, Schuylkill Co.-Chaplaincy

Schuylkill County VHC (from left) Lynn Samelko, Cecelia Pyzowski

Inner Mission/Com. Min. Schuylkill County (from left) Isabelle Hallock, Sally Reed, hospital visitor

135

VOLUNTEERS

Volunteering is a ministry of caring that happens at every facility and in every program. Many volunteers have become part of the extended family of many of the nursing care residents. They assist in arts and crafts activities, read to residents, or simply give someone a wheelchair ride.

Volunteer couples assist Family Life Services with premarriage workshops. They give presentations on select topics and serve as group discussion leaders.

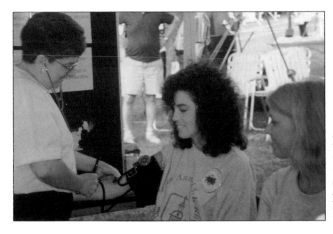

Home Health
Services
(from left)
Carolyn Heffner,
Donna Dietrich,
Kathy Lantz

Community Volunteers - The Board of Trustees is a very unique group of 30 volunteers who offer their time, talents, and treasure to The Lutheran Home. These men and women affect the direction and operations from year to year.

Many individuals and church and youth groups work year-round visiting the residents, accompanying them on trips and appointments, and helping with holiday decorations and parties. They worked for Anniversary Day, Week of Good News, and Christmas activities.

The day care children visit the Henry Infirmary residents, celebrate holidays together and serve as an important link with life.

Resident Volunteers - Residents help one another each day in countless ways. They deliver mail in the Luther Crest Health Care Center and Henry Infirmary. Residents manage and staff the gift shops, Luther Crest Library, and Topton Clothing Shoppe. They are involved in planning musical, cultural, and spiritual programs.

The Lutheran Home depends on volunteers to assist in maintaining and expanding its vital services. In 1994, the campuses of Allentown, Reading and Topton received more than 166,000 hours of service from almost 5,000 volunteers.

AUXILIARY

The Auxiliary of The Lutheran Home, organized on September 22, 1963, is the single largest group of volunteers supporting the campuses and programs. These men and women assist with Anniversary Day in July, serve as guides and train operators for the Christmas Putz. They also make financial contributions for furnishings and equipment.

During 1994, the Auxiliary provided over $6,300 to various programs and for equipment. The Auxiliary celebrated 33 years of service in 1995. During this time the Auxiliary, which has been so supportive, continued to be active and involved. The Auxiliary has been extremely helpful in expanding the volunteer program.

Auxiliary Presidents since its inception:

Bessie F. Moatz	1963-1967
Marian B. Heckman	1967-1971
Lorena W. Carlson	1971-1975
Amy H. Reinsel	1975-1979
LaRue P. Kieffer	1979-1983
Helen L. Emhardt	1983-1987
Betsy L. Moll	1987-1991
Helen Stimmel	1991-1995

RETIRED and SENIOR VOLUNTEER PROGRAM (RSVP)

In 1965, the Community Service Society of New York launched a pilot project on Staten Island called SERVE (Serve and Enrich Retirement by Volunteer Experience.) This project led to an amendment to the Older Americans Act, creating the Retired and Senior Volunteer Program (RSVP) in 1969. In 1993, The Lutheran Home at Topton obtained the contract for this program in Lehigh, Northampton and Carbon Counties.

RSVP offers older adults a meaningful life through volunteer service that is responsive to community needs. RSVP provides opportunities for persons age 55 and over to serve on a regular basis in a variety of settings throughout their communities. RSVP members serve in projects in all 50 states, Puerto Rico, the Virgin Islands and the District of

Columbia. Anyone age 55 or over is eligible to be an RSVP member. Persons with disabilities are welcome to serve.

BENEFACTORS' DINNERS

In 1988, The Lutheran Home began a Benefactors' Dinner as a fund-raiser. This is now an annual event and features a succession of nationally-known speakers. Average attendance is approximately 600 persons. In 1995, over $130,000 was netted!

EXPANSION

As expansion continued, it became obvious Pastor Buehrle needed help in specific and specialized areas. Therefore, Vice Presidents for Services to Aging, Community Ministries, Finance, Human Resources and Institutional Advancement were added to the staff as the needs arose.

· Public Relations department has received a number of awards for excellence for publications that told the story of The Lutheran Home's many services.

· Physical Therapy outpatient department has undergone considerable expansion.

· Commonwealth of Pennsylvania has approved The Lutheran Home to be a training ground for nurse aides.

This meets the requirement for special training. It provides certification needed by all of the individuals who provide nurses' aide service in long term care settings.

BRANDYWINE LIBRARY

· In continuing to show our interest in community partnerships, the Brandywine Library was housed on the Topton campus of The Lutheran Home at Topton as a gesture of goodwill and charity to the community. It is The Lutheran Home's way of being able to say 'thank you' for the support that the community has provided over the years.

CAPITAL CAMPAIGN

In 1993, the Board of Trustees voted to enter into its first-ever formalized capital campaign for The Lutheran Home at Topton. The campaign was designed to be conducted in Berks County, Lehigh County and Schuylkill County, the primary service delivery areas for The Lutheran Home at Topton. The campaign goal is $11.5 million, which includes new buildings, endowment enhancement and annual giving.

The buildings would be a new skilled nursing facility to replace the beds in an older section of the building on the Topton campus that still had 4 beds in a room. The new building would have a wing that would be considered a dementia unit to concentrate primarily on aiding victims of Alzheimer's Disease. The buildings that would be vacated would be converted to house 49 personal care beds and would be named the **Buehrle Personal Care Building** in honor of the Rev. Dr. Paul Buehrle.

SERVICE SUMMARY:

Housing for elderly	1,823
Senior Neighborhood Centers	1,195
Meals-On-Wheels	921
Volunteer Home Care	515
Latino Social Services/ Inner Mission	1,195
	5,649

ANNIVERSARY DAY

This celebration has adapted over the years. As you'll see in the next chapter, there were plays with "a cast of thousands! *(Well...the cast usually included ALL the children and staff!)* Those days are gone, but new attractions, such as a 5K race, the Anniversary Day Chorus and departmental exhibits attract attention and participation! Of course, there's always fine music, excellent food and an opportunity to meet and greet old and new friends.

A Gift of Love

How the service has multiplied. From the first two orphans, Sallie and Clair Carl in 1897...to over 5,600 served in 1995! When the search committee bought the Diener farm, could they have visualized the success which would come to this hilltop location? Perhaps.

When Rev. Heilman dug the foundation for the Old Main building in the shape of a cross, did he have an insight into how that act would turn into "A Gift of Love?" Perhaps.

Remember, these hard-working people DID have the vision and fortitude a century ago. Their faith was as strong as their love of family and country. They just 'took it on faith' and began an incredible project. And they did have the 'inner vision' and faith to set out boldly.

Here is an aerial view of just PART of their dream come true, the Topton campus. The full scope of operations stretches over thousands of square miles and tens of thousands of people in eastern Pennsylvania.

Topton Campus

142

When this book began, it started with a few pages of notes of my conversation with Pastor Buehrle in his office. Recently, I returned with the almost-completed manuscript, plus boxes overflowing with photos, notes, etc.

It was late afternoon, and his telephone list kept growing. He motioned to me to bring my tablet and we snuck out...just to the front porch. We sat and looked out over the panorama. A train whistle called mournfully. A flock of testy crows announced themselves to all who would listen.

There is hardly any human activity that cannot be improved by a few minutes of quiet contemplation of this magnificent view. Neither of us spoke for quite a while. Then I asked him, "What does the future hold for The Lutheran Home at Topton?"

Pastor got up, looked out and collected his thoughts. He said that he feels the challenge of the future is:

. maintaining what we have

. upgrading to meet (and anticipate) competition

. maintain nursing quality
(beds will always be needed)

We talked about how, in the past, the Lutherans were proud of being able to handle all the challenges without asking for outside help.

"Things are much different now," he noted. He anticipates joint ventures, plus more cooperative ventures in our eastern and central Pennsylvania service area. He predicts that "the health care system will be reconfigured, with total coverage for everyone."

I asked if he thought that The Lutheran Home was ready for the next century...the second 100 years. Again, there was a long pause. He replied, "I feel that truly outstanding progress has been made and that we are well-positioned for the next century...a strong organization, serving people. In my opinion, this is because of a forward-looking Board, willing to take many risks and a full staff of unique employees willing to be faithful to the task."

One can't be with Pastor Buehrle very long without hearing about how grateful he has been for all the volunteers, the support of staff and excellent Board representation over these 20 years. Without their competence, he is convinced that The Lutheran Home would not be as great as it has turned out to be. He feels blessed to have been a part of this excellent organization.

He is grateful that he's had the opportunity to join the list of those who have gone before and who have worked with him, and also to have been honored by Muhlenberg College in 1981 with a Doctor of Divinity degree.

The few moments on the porch came to an end, as people discovered our hiding place. He turned to me, took one last look at the campus and said, "A Gift of Love. Wonderful name for the book. This whole hundred years has been a gift of love."

Chapter 9

WHAT WAS IT LIKE...?

Our readers probably have two questions:

1. What was the real history of The Lutheran Home?

2. What was it like to be an orphan here?

The first eight chapters attempt to compress 100 years of history into one slender volume. And, while it's fascinating history, parts of the history **have** been publicized over the years in newspapers and other media. Additionally, thousands of people have come to the Anniversary Day celebrations, begun as Donation Day on August 16, 1900. So, most of us know SOMETHING about The Lutheran Home

But, while the Orphans' Home Paper and The Herald did chronicle the story of "what's going on" in faithful, accurate and eloquent form, the circulation was not very large. Therefore, only 1,618 people (the orphans themselves) and the staff really knew exactly what it was like to live here.

Now it's our turn. We've collected some remembrances here for you, along with some pictures from 'way back when.' You'll read: (a) the rules and regulations of what it was SUPPOSED to be like and (b) what it was REALLY like, including what the meals were like. The final remembrance is an incredible chronicle by Marian Heckman. This is truly 'living history.'

Come and see what life was REALLY like in words and pictures of another time!

March 1897. In all our activities here at the Orphans' Home, we maintain a religious atmosphere. They hear no swearing, neither foul and smutty speech. They are taught to pray daily, are instructed to the way of salvation, must commit the Catechism and many

*Christian hymns to memory. They receive a fair
common school education and are taught to work in
the house and on the farm. They get a fair start for life
and heaven. Orphans' Homes have been an
incalculable blessing to many poor boys and girls.*

*June 1905 - PRESIDENT'S REPORT: There are now 68
orphans here. The health of these is good; during the
winter, however, many of them suffered from colds,
sore throats, and some from pneumonia; there were no
less than fifteen down at one time.*

*The Superintendent and his estimable wife are doing
good and aggressive work among the children. The
boys are taught to work on the farm and in the
workshop, and the girls to do housework. Everyone is
expected to do a certain prescribed portion of work
each day. On Saturday scrubbing the halls, steps and
floors is added to their daily routine.*

*To divide the work evenly, and in proportion to age
and size, also to secure more satisfactory results, a
schedule has been prepared which is followed very
carefully. The children are divided into eight groups,
each consisting of four boys and four girls. Each group
is in charge of the older children. The Building is also
divided into eight sections.*

*Each of these groups serves in a section one month, and
changes to another on the first of every month. The
girls going from the kitchen to the dining room, from
the dining room to the halls and from there to the
bedrooms. The boys follow the same routine on their
side of the house. The older girls are also taught the
requirements of a family kitchen, such as cooking,
baking and preparing meals, especially on Saturday
and Sunday.*

*The religious training of the children receives a great
deal of care. They are taught in the Bible, Luther's
Catechism, and in addition they commit to memory a*

number of the best hymns. In Sunday-school the graded system of the General Council is used.

Their course of study generally is similar to that of the public schools, and is in charge of two competent teachers. The results of their work is very satisfactory. Last summer Dr. N. C. Schaeffer, State Superintendent of Public Schools, appointed Profs. Ira Shipman, of Sunbury, and A. K. Rutt, of Milton on the examining committee at the K. S. N. School. They visited our Home and assisted in properly grading our schools.

These gentlemen report: "We spent some time in the school, presided over by two teachers. It was on the last day of the term, but the schoolwork was in progress the same as we would have expected during the middle of the term, thus giving evidence that neither time nor opportunity is lost. The teaching gives evidence of careful intellectual, aesthetic, moral and religious training. We were especially impressed with discipline and moral tone of the school. The children seem to act from principle and right teaching, not because they were watched over, or because of fear. We examined them in their work. The test showed that they were instructed by approved methods and to good purpose. Not only are the common school subjects taught proficiently, but much attention is also paid to music. The children are also carefully instructed along moral and religious lines."

Feb. 1909 - HOME ITEMS, We are sure it will be of interest to learn about a day's life at our Home. The many relatives and friends of the children who are inmates of this place must surely speak of our large family quite often and would like to know how a day's life really goes on. The day begins in the morning, and every business man starts his day's duties in the morning, The same is also true at our Home, as a great deal of work is connected herewith. Our life here must go like clockwork. If not, we would never get through

*and never have order, therefore our rising bell rings at
6 o'clock in the morning, and all the children and
employees must arise punctually.*

*From 6 until 6:30 the children wash and dress, and at
6:30 the bell rings again for the morning service, when
all assemble in the schoolroom for a short devotional
service. As this Home is located in a German section,
we last spring introduced the German language, too,
therefore, our morning service is conducted in German.*

*We sing two verses of the hymn, "Nun danket alle Gott"
("Now Thank We All Our God"), after which we read a
chapter from a devotional book, followed by a
morning prayer and the Lord's Prayer. We then close
with last verse of the same hymn and the benediction.
Immediately after this service the children go to their
dormitories and make their beds under the supervision
of a grown person.*

*At 7 o'clock the breakfast bell rings, when all march in
single file, girls and boys respectively, to the dining
room, and go to their appointed places at the tables.
The bell is tapped and all take seats and repeat in
unison the German prayer, "Aller Augen warten auf
dich Herr" ("All eyes wait upon Thee, O Lord"),*

*After Breakfast, about twenty minutes, they leave the
dining room and go to their dormitories and do their
work, such as sweeping and dusting, the oldest girls
clearing the tables and washing the dishes, while the
smallest ones play.*

*Since last winter we taught the children German and
Bible history from 8 to 9 o'clock in the morning so as
not the interfere with the school schedule.*

*At 9 o'clock the school bell rings, and all the children
gather in the school room, open with song and prayer
and then go to their lessons. From 10:30 until 10:45
they have a recess period, when all partake of a little*

lunch, as an apple, or a piece of bread, etc. At 11:45 school closes for the morning, and at the same time the first dinner bell rings. The older girls go to the kitchen and help with dinner, while the rest wash and prepare for dinner.

Promptly at 12 the dinner bell rings again, all march in as in the morning, say grace and eat. After dinner the children go to play until quarter of 1, when the first school bell rings. They then prepare for school. At 1 o'clock the bell rings again and all go to their classes. From 2:30 until 2:45 the recess period takes place, accompanied with a little lunch. Then from 2:45 until 4 o'clock school is in session.

From 4 until 6 the time is spent in playing, preparing lessons, and assisting in the kitchen, as well as in the sewing room. At 6 o'clock the supper bell rings and all enjoy the last meal of the day. After supper, the girls help in the kitchen, while others play, and at 7 o'clock the little tots go to bed.

At 7: 30 the evening worship bell rings, and all again assemble in the main schoolroom for service. This consists of a hymn, reading of a psalm, reading of a chapter from a devotional book, Lord's Prayer, an Evening Prayer and benediction.

At 8 o'clock the middle-aged children go the bed. From 8 to 9 we instruct the children in choir singing or catechism. At 9 o'clock everyone is expected to retire, and the house father goes from room to room to see that all are well and asleep in their tiny beds.

Uh-oh! You just went to sleep and everyone's getting dressed. What's this commotion? It's a parade of at least two hundred people, coming up Home Avenue towards the Lutheran Orphans' Home.

Put yourself in the picture in a kinder, gentler era...don't you wish we had THIS one on video?

May 1910 - ONE HUNDRED AND SIX POUND
SOUR BALL FOR THE ORPHANS
On Tuesday evening, April 13, a sourball weighing 106
pounds was presented to the orphans by Frank J.
Dierolf and James Biery, of Topton. The sourball was
the feature of a parade in town which caused many
spectators to join the procession to the Home. The
procession was headed by Herbert Hoppes and George
Kunkle in a buggy, the latter holding the sourball. The
Schweyers Band and about 200 men, women and
children were in procession.

The older children in study hour, the younger ones were
in bed. Some were not asleep, however, and when told
what was going on it took a very short time for them to
get dressed. They all went on the front porch to listen to
the band music. After one selection, they all went to the
school room, where it was suggested by the Topton
people that we break the ball in the their presence.
Chas. Seaman, our oldest boy, had the honor to break
it. It was delicious and was enjoyed immensely by the
children. We are so glad to think that the good people
of Topton have a warm heart for our dear orphans. It
is encouraging to live in a community where the people
are in sympathy with the work.

FOOD

This description is reprinted as it was received. We're not
sure of the author, but the guess is the woman who was in
charge of the kitchen at the Home, possibly in the 1920's.
The writing style starts out stiffly, as if someone DID make
her write it all down. Then, she warms to her task, willing to
share truly fascinating details. For instance, "Bread for the
small children is spread in the kitchen, and not spread too
thick with butter either." Can you see her wagging her
finger as she talks?

Yes, it's of another age, but the love, caring and fairness
shine through. It is as if we walked into her large kitchen,
surrounded with wonderful smells, and asked her to tell us

about her work. Sit back and listen to her caring voice speak to you over the years, as she discusses:

For such a large family, one naturally might expect it would take a large amount of food for each meal. Care must be taken that no food is wasted, that thrift and economy be practiced insofar as it is consistent with the health of the children. Growing children require certain foods, particularly those adapted to their particular needs.

Then again, the State Laws to a great degree, control the kinds of food to be used, the manner of their preparation, and the quantity to be given to each child. This is especially true in reference to milk and butter and fruit.

We try to prepare good wholesome food, serve it nicely, and give everybody a sufficient quantity. No distinction is shown between the children and employees. No set menus are followed so that no one knows what they may expect on certain days of the week, as is done in many institutions as well as in some homes.

For instance, Monday is not always Sauer Kraut Day, detested by some and liked by others. I will try and give you an idea of the kind of food, the quantities used, etc.

For example, for breakfast:

Oatmeal	*2-20 quart boilers*
Bread & Butter	*25 loaves of bread*
Cocoa	*Half milk generally*

Applesauce and prunes, or some kind of fruit, usually two bushels of apples are used when they make apple sauce, two bushels for baked apples. Bread for the small children is spread in the kitchen, and not spread too thick with butter either.

For dinner:

Most dinners are boiled dinners, that is, 50 lbs. of boiled beef with:

Potatoes and turnips:	*2 bu. for a meal*
Potatoes and cabbage	*2 bu. for a meal*
Beans, string Pot-pie	*Sauer Kraut*

Occasionally vegetable soup is served as the main dish for dinner, and bread and apple butter.

On Sundays roast meat is served, usually pork or beef, sometimes chicken, especially in the fall, when the flock of chickens is culled. Twenty-two to twenty-five chickens to a meal. Also ice cream (made from milk) is served for dessert.

For supper:

Mush and milk	*Bread, and Molasses or Jelly*
Rice and milk	*Brown potato soup*
Rivel soup	

Leftovers from dinner are always eaten first for supper, divided among different tables each day. Pie once a week, and cake once a week, such as shoofly, cocoanut cake, or its equivalent. Sunday supper small cakes are served.

Author's note: We have tried to use photographs not published before. You'll note that many are 'group photos' (to be expected.) Almost none are identified in the records. The photos do not go with the anecdotes; they have their own story to tell.

Probably three incoming boys.

"Well, I'm all dressed up,
so let's go!"

"OK…on three…
get the photographer…
one…two…"

Holton
Memorial
'family.'

A Gift of Love

Topton Station:
Highest point
between Philadelphia
and Reading, hence
the town's name.

An excellent method
of transportation,
as you'll read!

The Ice Rink:
Original
farmhouse
in back,
kids having a
great time
in front!

The mowers:
Check out:
. knickers
. shirts & ties
. the push-pull
  'team' in
  the middle

154

Easter Baskets:
And this is just
a portion of
the group!

The Baby Choir:
There are DOZENS of photos of these
children over the decades. They loved
to sing. Photographers loved to 'take
just one more!'

However, almost every photo shows the
children in the Baby Choir looking
"everywhere but at the camera."
(But they ARE cute, aren't they?)

The "Middie Look"
hits campus!

A Gift of Love

Off to school! (Do you get the feeling that the photographer was EVERYWHERE?)

"I picked these flowers for you! Aren't they pretty?"

Ladies and gentlemen... start your engines!

Sadie (Baus) Walker 1925-1939

The happiest day of my life was Dec. 9, 1939. Rev. Henry married Robert and Sadie (Baus) Walker in the Home chapel and all the children were invited to the wedding. Afterward, "all" had home-made cake and ice cream. I think that was the first wedding many of the children had seen. It is now 56 years later and we are still married and happy. This was the best thing I can share.

Besides the obvious 'choreography' directions from the photographer, these photos are interesting for the many different expressions on the faces from so many years ago. The little girls above are primarily squinting into the sun, but the older boys' faces seem to reveal secrets about their view of life and the future.

William E. Derrick 1924-1936

I didn't realize that those were the Great Depression years! Living with 100 boys and 100 girls didn't give much time to worry about the outside world.

Our administrators DID keep reminding us to conserve, because many people out there were suffering economic distress. These same people were trying to help us with their meager contributions. Years later, we look back and smile at our escapades!

SHARE!

If a visiting friend or relative gave one of us a candy bar, we'd cut it into at least ten pieces to share with the host of friends who appeared by magic at the sound of the wrapper crinkling! We did learn to share...an important trait. *Remember that in those days, a 5c candy bar was bigger than today's 50c version.*

Once in a while, one of the boys would have a rich uncle or aunt who'd buy him a pair of roller skates ($2 at Sears, Roebuck & Co.) These skates were kept rolling all day, first by the owner, then he lent them to a friend, then a second friend, and so on until the ball-bearings fell out of some of the wheels.

The good wheels were reclaimed and fastened onto a couple of pieces of wood, which produced a scooter! The scooter was run all day until IT failed, then all the ball-bearings were reclaimed as ammunition for home-made slingshots. They were made from innertubes found on the junkpile. That great junkpile was the source of lots of great inventions!

HOW TO HIDE STUFF

All of the boys wore blouses which buttoned at the waist. These blouses not only shielded our bodies from the elements, but they also served as a carrying pouch for all sorts of necessary things, such as apples, pears, plums and all kinds of small toys.

There were all kinds of handy fruit trees on the premises. We didn't hesitate to pick up a nice looking piece of fruit.

NICKNAMES

Most of the boys earned a nickname, usually bestowed on them for a physical feature, something they did or anything WE considered abnormal. For example, here's how one fellow received his nickname.

He was standing on the porch, sounding off in a high-pitched yodel type of holler, when the Superintendent, Rev. Henry, walked up to him and asked what the hollering was all about. He answered, "I'm listening to my echo down through the woods." Rev. Henry told him that he was checking him out to determine whether or not he was having a problem. From that day on, his nickname (of course) became "Echo."

Likewise a fellow, who got caught stealing a can of baked beans, was forever called "Beans." One Sunday morning, one of the older boys was asked to read the scripture lesson during church service. You guessed it! From that Sunday on, he was known on campus as "Preacher."

TEMPTATION

We were supposed to turn in any money received from friends or relatives. This was put into our individual savings account and was returned to us upon being discharged from the care of the Lutheran Orphans Home.

However...we learned that there were some candy and ice-cream stores just off campus which posed a temptation. One day as he was looking from his office window, Rev. Henry saw three boys leaving campus for exactly that reason. They were too far away to identify without binoculars. The next day, he asked one of the neighbors who lived just on the edge of the Home's premises if he saw three boys headed for the candy store last evening.

The neighbor said he did, but didn't know their real names. He could, however, give him their nicknames. That evening, in the assembly room, Rev. Henry announced that he wanted **Digger, Flops** and **Knack** to come to his office. All the boys knew EXACTLY who he was looking for.

The amusing part is that Rev. Henry had no idea whom to expect until the three boys came forward. We often wondered why he never got to know our nicknames...we shouted them back and forth many times over!

CELEBRATIONS

As children, we always looked forward to holidays. They were full of pleasing, appropriate programs and EVERYONE took part. No one was anxious to appear on stage, but this was our first opportunity to deal with stage fright. Some people can conquer it, others don't. Such plays and performances gave our teachers a chance to check out our capabilities and gave US many learning experiences.

Besides celebrating the national holidays, we had four annual celebrations of our own, which included 100% participation among the children, staff members and employees. On the first Saturday in March, Mrs. Henry and her staff planned and arranged one big birthday party to celebrate EVERYONE's birthday. On our actual birthdate, we were entitled to the same number of cookies to match our age. *No one was concerned about their age at that time!*

On July Fourth, there was a big picnic on campus for everyone to enjoy. It consisted of hot dogs, sodas, candy, games and races. Sometimes an outside friend of the family would set off some firecrackers for our enjoyment. On Hallowe'n, we had one big Hallowe'n party with plenty of fresh apple cider. We each received a big candy apple, and we played games and ran races for prizes. We made our own false faces from paper, cardboard and rags, and there was an extra prize for the best false face.

For New Year's, we had a special party consisting of home made ice cream, home made peanut taffy, homemade chocolate caramels, plus soda pop, pretzels and potato chips.

TAKE OUT THE GARBAGE

Mealtimes were punctual and everyone ate at the same time. After over 200 people have eaten a meal including watermelon and corn on the cob, a veritable mountain of garbage is produced.

One day, two of us boys were selected to carry the garbage out to the pigs. After dumping it on the ground in the center of the pig pen, Johnny decided to ride one of the pigs. He jumped on, the pig bolted forward, and JOHNNY landed PRECISELY in the middle of the slop pile! On the way back to the main building, we had to stop at the creek to wash his clothes. It was a very embarrassing situation that evening, but now we can both smile at the humor.

THE OUTSIDE WORLD

Living in such a sheltered environment gave us our own perception of the outside world. As we got older and learned to read, we had access to the <u>Reading Eagle</u> and the <u>Allentown Morning Call</u> newspapers, which were passed around from one department to another. However, there were those few who <u>were</u> naive enough to believe that Ivory Soap is made from elephant tusks!

It wasn't hard to believe that everyone on the outside was a Lutheran. Likewise, some thought that the thousands of people who appeared on Anniversary Day were all the people in Pennsylvania!

Yes, those were the days, my friend; we thought they'd never end...but they did. Nevertheless, those memories will live on forever. I'm glad I was privileged to live the experience. Who would have suspected that a financially poor boy would come away from The Lutheran Home at Topton, PA so rich in wisdom, friendships and memories? I will always cherish those memories.

Ice Skating Secrets: A closer look reveals that the 'skaters' seem to be just 'skidders'. There is some imaginative headgear!

A Gift of Love

Virginia (Baer) Ebersole (1933-1946)

Memories:

White dresses on Anniversary Day...Christmas Morning with John C. Cook's German Band...Rainy Sunday afternoons watching Popeye movies...Sunday evenings, walking through the flower gardens...sitting on the front steps at sunset, looking over the entire valley view and singing "Day is Dying in the West."

Hot pepper! Hot pepper!

Rev. Henry and a confirmation class.

Donald A. Gum (1930-1946)

BABY CHOIR

From the first time I can remember, I was a member of the "Baby Choir." This is when I first began to sing. Music was taught to us in the grade school and was an important part of our learning and growing up.

Singing in the adult choir, school plays, plays put on for church groups and Anniversary Day were all important activities. Once I left the Home, I continued to sing in church choirs. I even sang during my 24 years of military service. Even now, 65 years later, I still sing in our church choir. I must give much credit to my upbringing at the Home and thank the Lord that the Home was there for me and my brothers and sisters.

FORBIDDEN FRUIT

Every year during Spring and Fall cleaning, we looked forward to cleaning out the fruit cellar. This was the basement room where the canned and jarred fruit was stored. It was our chance to get canned fruit for ourselves. The fellows really enjoyed it, *especially* if it was gotten 'illegally.'

During the cleaning process, we'd put jars of fruit into our bucket of dirty water, then go to 'dump out this dirty water and get some clean water.' We'd take the long route which happened to pass through our locker room, where we'd hide the jar. It had also been washed off nicely during its little trip! Also, there were pipes across the ceiling and through the walls, with space enough for a jar or two. Later, we'd come back and to enjoy the sweet fruit.

LITTLE DEVILS

When we were about 10 or 11, we slept in the middle dormitory on the second floor. This was the bedroom for boys. The janitor, Mr. Derrick, had his room next to our dormitory. Whenever we were in a devilish mood, one of the boys would throw a shoe against his door. This would continue until he would storm out of his room with a strap or stick and go down the row of beds, batting at where our legs were supposed to be. Heh. We'd pull our feet up as high as we could, and we'd holler "ouch" real loud to make him satisfied that he hit us. That would be that for the night.

When we picked potatoes out in the field, if a nest of mice was disturbed, we'd chase them, then stomp them with our bare feet. They always got away in the soft ground. We would also wait for the tractor to come by, then put our foot under the wheel. Since it was a large rubber tire and the ground was soft, nothing ever happened. It was just another dare from the kids.

GARDENS

Springtime was also a busy time for Mrs. Henry. Not only was she busy with her own gardens, which provided flowers for the Chapel and Dining Room tables, she also saw to it that the boys and girls had gardens of their own. Every Spring, small plots were marked off for each girl and boy to have a vegetable and flower garden.

When the vegetables were ripe, the kids were allowed to bring them in and sell them. Rev. Henry would pay whatever price he thought was right. A little bargaining took place, too. This way, we learned about the price of food and groceries early.

NEITHER RAIN, NOR SNOW...

Now that I live in Gulfport, Mississippi, I often think back to the times when I walked the road from the Home to the Topton Post Office. I carried and picked up the mail for the Home every day except Sunday, regardless of rain, snow or temperature. Summer wasn't bad, even when it rained. Winters WERE harsh, especially in a wind-driven snowstorm. Going to and from the Post Office took 30-45 minutes. I'll always remember.

During the school year, as soon as I brought the mail back, I had to turn around and go back to town where I attended Junior High School. Walking kept me in good physical shape. I look back now on those days as a learning and growing experience.

One thing that amazed me was the construction of the (George E. Holton Cottage) baby cottage. As a little boy (age 1 to 4), the building seemed like a normal house. After growing up and coming back to the cottage, I felt like a giant! I never knew this cottage was built on a smaller scale for little children. Even the furniture was made for little folks. My grandfather made half a dozen rocking chairs for us to play with. I appreciate the fact that this building, where lots of love abounded every day, was made to accommodate little children.

WATCH FOR "STUBBY"

One of our favorite delivery men was "Stubby the Baker." "Stubby" delivered baked goods to the farmers in the area; we KNEW his route. When we were working in the fields, we'd wait for him to come by. Or we'd send someone to one of his stops, so we could buy sweet rolls. We had to pool our change so we had enough, but somehow "Stubby" always gave us more than we could afford. I'm sure he saw to it that he had extras on his truck. He was always on the lookout for us, even though he knew it was against the rules.

THE CORNFIELD 'LONG BALL CAPER'

Getting ice cream was another challenge. The ball fields were located below the Home. Next to that was the cornfield. While playing baseball, we'd do our best to hit a ball into the cornfield. The outfielder would have to disappear into the cornfield to get the ball. The ball would come flying back, but his assignment was to keep right on going into town to the ice-cream store. When he'd get back, via the cornfield, we'd share the ice cream with each other. Of course, we were always on the lookout for the Reverend. If we got caught, it would be awhile 'til we played ball again!

A Gift of Love

Everybody's off to have fun on a trip to Carsonia Park in Reading!

And how would YOU like to organize this event, hm?

It's the famous "Blue Beetle!

LUTHERAN ORPHANS' HOME
TOPTON, PENNA.

All aboard the
Good Health Express!"

The Putz
was always
fascinating!

Memories...

A Gift of Love

Author's Note: Kenneth J. Boldt is the secretary of The Lutheran Home at Topton Alumni Association. At the Alumni Association annual meeting on May 29, 1995, he showed me a huge scrapbook he constructed for his granddaughter. While he wrote this poignant story just for her, he has allowed us to reprint it in this volume.

Kenneth J. Boldt (1931-1943)

My story begins in October, 1930. These were hard times in the whole country. We were in the midst of what they called "The Big Depression." Many people were out of work. They had a hard time to get money to support their families. All they thought of was to get enough money to buy food for their table and pay the rent.

I lived at 1040 Spruce Street in Reading, PA. My family included three brothers and two sisters. My youngest sister was just born on October 12, 1931. Seven days later, on October 19th, our mother died. I was five years old at that time. This was a sad time for me. At that age, I did not understand why this could happen. What was going to happen to all of us? The one person, who I am told, was the real backbone of the family, had died.

Well, as you will learn in my story to you, this was happening all over the country. Fathers and mothers were dying; and, in some cases, both parents were lost. What was to happen to all of these children? Aunts and uncles of these families had enough problems of their own, so they could not take these children.

But the churches were concerned about these families and their children who needed help. So, the church orphanages sprang up throughout the country It was their answer to a growing problem: "What do we do to help these children?"

TAKEN TO THE LUTHERAN ORPHANS' HOME

In the spring of 1931, I remember being dressed to be taken to such an orphanage. It was called The Lutheran Orphans' Home at Topton. What made the situation even worse was that our family was being separated. My older brother and sister would be staying in Reading with my father. My brother, Robert (one year younger than me) was being taken to live with another family, with the possibility that they would adopt him.

My brother, Carl, and sister, Betty, and myself; were taken that day by car to a place called Topton. It was out in the country. There was a large main building; also a Junior Boy's Cottage, a Junior Girl's Cottage, a Baby Cottage, a school house and an infirmary for the sick.

Carl and Betty were placed in the baby cottage, and I was placed in the junior boy's cottage, as I was only five years old. I was devastated. My family had been all split up. I was in this cottage with about twenty other boys, all of us about the same age. There were two matrons who had charge of this cottage. They saw to our personal care. They fed us, bathed us, washed our clothes, mended our clothes. They did whatever was necessary to make us comfortable in our new home.

Over a period of time, I adjusted to living in this new environment. We all related to each other. We became like brothers, as we had all suffered the loss of one or both parents. As new children came to the "Home," you eventually became one of the "older" kids. As an older boy, (eight or nine years old) you moved to the main building.

LIFE IN THE MAIN BUILDING

The main building was divided in half. The west side was for the girls. There was an invisible barrier (right down the middle) which neither side would cross. Boys and girls only got together on special occasions. These occasions included the Fourth of July, Everybody's birthday party, etc. We also were together for morning and evening worship in the east wing, and church on Sundays in the chapel on the west wing. Brothers and sisters could come to "the line" and talk with each other, but we couldn't cross the line.

Living in the main building was quite different than the cottages. You had to care for yourself, such as washing and bathing. The older boys made sure the younger ones were properly dressed, shoes tied, and all of those personal things.

Also, in the main building, you were given a number. This was your number until you left the "Home". My number was 53. Your clothing was all marked with your number. Your mirror in the washroom had your number above it. This is where your towel was hung. Your coat and hat were hung on your hook in the cellar. Your hook had your number above it. Directly below your coat were your rubbers for your shoes. Everything was kept neat and orderly.

We had a large playroom with large tables and chairs. Two of the walls were covered with large blackboards. There also were two player pianos and bookcases filled with books, such as the Tom Swift series and Rover Boys. There were between fifty and sixty boys living in this large area.

There was also a special room off to the side. It was called the Big Boy's Reading Room. You could not enter this room until you were confirmed. This room was just for the older boys to be by themselves. The room also contained a player piano, many bookcases and also a small radio.

The boy's side had three bedrooms. The smaller one was for the younger boys. In the west wing, above the chapel, was another bedroom, used for those who had a bed-wetting problem. This was done so the bedding could be washed and aired out properly.

On the third floor, under the tower's dome, was a huge room. This was called the Big Boy's Bedroom. There was no heat up to the third floor, so in the winter it got <u>really</u> cold up there. The floors were bare except for rugs that ran down the aisles between the rows of beds. We were warm because we had plenty of covers.

OUR DAILY ROUTINE

The morning bell rang at 6:00 a.m.. We got out of bed, got dressed and went down to the washroom to wash and brush our teeth. Morning worship was at 6:30 a.m.. We walked by twos to the east wing, where we sang a hymn, read a passage of scripture and had a prayer by the Superintendent.

After morning worship, we assembled in our washrooms. Then, when the dining room door was opened, we went in by twos to our place at the table. After breakfast, we filed out to our washrooms to wash our face and hands.

After that, we were assigned jobs, which were our daily duties. You might have swept with a broom, mopped, dusted or washed windows. Every part of our quarters was cleaned daily.

In the wintertime, then, it was off to school. In the summertime, it was working on the outside.

There was grass to cut, hedges to trim, a vegetable patch to hoe, work to be done on the farm. There was plenty to do to keep you busy. Dinner was served at noon, and after dinner, it was back to work details. Supper was served at 5:00 p.m. After supper, you had time to yourself to relax. During school, this was the time for studies. Evening worship was at 7:00 p.m. Basically it was the same as morning worship - hymn, scripture, and a prayer.

There was time left to study and relax until bedtime at 9:00 p.m. The older boys could stay up until 10:00 p.m. This routine continued day after day, year after year. There was very little change except for holidays.

CHRISTMAS CELEBRATIONS

Holidays were always special days. There were lots of preparations. Christmas was one of the biggest holidays at the "Home." In November, we started to collect moss in the woods to be used for the shepherd's scene for the "Putz". It was a gigantic Christmas yard.

One-third of the display was for the Christmas story from the Bible. The rest of the space was for trains, West Point on parade, and a lot of other various scenes. There was also a biplane that hung from the ceiling.

Then we also had to prepare for our program on Christmas Eve. This was always the Christmas story as told in the Bible. Each child received only one present on Christmas day. A church would take the list of children and try to get a present for each of us.

Christmas day started early. The morning bell rang at 6:00 a.m. There was morning worship at 6:30 a.m. Then at 7:00 a.m., usually Cook's Pennsylvania German Band arrived to entertain the children. There was music and laughter. Then we had breakfast and there was our present on our plate.

After breakfast, we could play with our presents and see what everyone else had received. Soon it was dinnertime. Our Christmas dinner was always turkey. These were provided by Mr. Levi Long. We all had plenty to eat.

We spent the afternoon playing. We also enjoyed getting fruit and candy from the church groups that visited the "Home." The buildings were all decorated with trees that we cut from the woods. They were covered with lights and ornaments. Christmas was very special to us.

"EVERYBODY'S BIRTHDAY"

The next big holiday that I remember was a Saturday in March. The day was called "Everybody's Birthday Party." There were so many children, so everyone had a happy birthday on that day.

The employees and the older boys and girls put on a funny play. Then we had time for games and treats. There were homemade caramels and walnut taffy. It was always a real fun day.

EASTER

On Easter Sunday, we each had an Easter basket on our plate in the dining room. There were hard-boiled eggs, dyed with onion skins. They were all colored brown. We also did our Easter pageant in the afternoon. This was always the Easter story told in the Bible.

MEMORIAL DAY

Before you knew it, Spring was here. Then, it was Memorial Day. What a day that was! Many of the kids that lived here before me would come back to visit. They told stories of their life on the outside world.

Many of the boys slept overnight in the big boys' bedroom.

The Alumni and the "Home" kids had their annual baseball game. It was always loads of fun.

FOURTH OF JULY

To celebrate the Fourth of July, flags were placed all over the grounds. We all ate dinner in the basement of the baby cottage. It was the one day of the year we were allowed to eat all the hot dogs that we could. We also got a bottle of soda pop.

ANNIVERSARY DAY

Then, there was the third Thursday in August, which was Anniversary Day. There was a lot of preparation. Stands had to be set up. They had canvas tops. The planks in the pavillion had to be placed. Various foods were prepared. Churches served dinners in various parts of the buildings. The bandstand had to be erected. We had our final re-hearsal of the pageant, which was performed that afternoon.

On the big day, people came by trains, cars and buses. They came by the thousands. The orphans were all dressed in white that day. You could pick us out in the crowd. The people were very kind to us and would give us treats or even money. At one o'clock in the afternoon, we all assembled in the chapel in the west wing.

Then, we marched down - two by two- to the pavillion to present the afternoon program. We were led by the band, which was at the head of the procession. After the program, we were free to do what we wished.

Usually, my father came that day. So, Betty, Carl and I spent the rest of the day with him. The next few days were spent taken everything down and cleaning up the grounds. We looked for money that people had dropped as we cleaned up all the paper that was there from Anniversary Day.

The rest of the summer was spent working on the farm. There were many crops to be harvested and stored for the winter. On the farm, there was wheat and oats to harvest; potatoes and corn to be stored. The apples had to be picked from the trees.

SCHOOL DAYS

Summer passed all too quickly. The swimming pool was closed. Now it was time for school. The "Home" had its own schoolhouse on campus. But they only taught up to eighth grade. They had four teachers and each teacher had four grades in their rooms.

When we finished school at the "Home", we went to Topton for ninth and tenth grades. To finish school, we had to travel to Kutztown on the school bus for eleventh and twelfth grades. Shortly after graduation, we left the "Home" to live in Reading with our father.

HALLOWEE'N

Fall was very pretty at the "Home." The trees were beautiful in their Autumn colors. Soon, October was here and that brought on Hallowee'n. The party was held in the main hall of the orphanage. We would dress up in our costumes, which we made ourselves. We'd all assemble in the big hall. It was a fun time for all.

It was soon time to make preparations for Christmas. There was always plenty to do at the "Home". When you were young, you had a lot of time to play. But once you were fourteen or older, you had a lot of work and responsibilities. We always had plenty of food to eat.

We also raised a lot of our own food on the farm and in our truck patch. We raised all kinds of vegetables. There were string beans, carrots, peas, corn, potatoes, etc. It took a lot of hoeing by hand, pulling weeds daily. There was cultivating with our horses, and plowing and all that was necessary. It was a good learning experience.

In the summertime we went without shoes to save leather. We learned to do with a lot less than the children of today. You were taught that you had responsibilities in this life, and your daily work assignments were a good lesson, which you eventually accepted.

In many of our assignments, whether on the farm or the chicken houses, you learned that you were responsible for these tasks. With all of us kids working together, we got a lot accomplished. But there were also times when you would rather do something else than work; after all, we were kids and there were always the times you would shirk your responsibilities. If you were caught doing that, you were punished, but it was fun trying to get ahead of Rev. Henry. But he almost always seemed to catch us.

TEMPTATIONS

There were places in the main building cellar that held our young minds in fascination. There was the fruit cellar, where all the jarred fruits were stored on shelves. That was a real challenge to get into the fruit cellar to taste those sweets.

There was also the wine barrels all in a row. We would tap out the cider and fill it with water. We were tricky at times and if we got caught, we had to take our punishment.

Money was scarce at the "Home." We were not supposed to keep money. If our relatives gave us money, we were supposed to turn it in at the office and it was recorded in the book behind our names.

But we used to keep it and not tell anyone. That way we had a little bit to spend whenever we could. If we had a nickel or a dime, we would stop the Topton baker on his route. We would stop him behind the chicken houses so Rev. Henry would not catch us. We called the driver "Stubby." He always had some stale cakes and buns to sell us for our nickels and dimes.

Lots of times we would sneak down to Topton, where one of the stores had penny candy. We were not supposed to leave the campus. Of course if we got caught, we would surely be punished.

It was a very secluded lifestyle and as you got older, you were curious about the world outside. As a teenager, we really started to wonder about life.

Girls became a big problem for us to cope with. Of course at the orphanage, you were never allowed to mingle with the opposite sex. The upstairs had that darn invisible dividing line right down the middle.

LOVE

That mystical thing called love. That first kiss when no one was looking! Oh, what a challenge that was. It seemed to be the greatest thing in the world. But that was all part of growing up.

As an "older boy," I took part in 'tending kids.' This was helping out in the cottages where the small children lived. My chore was to take out the garbage from the pantry. The matron, Mrs. Kleckner, had five daughters. One of them was in my grade in school, so we knew each other. On the weekend, she would take over for her mother.

So, she'd be washing dishes and I'd come by to take out the garbage. I'd go in the pantry, call out: "Is this everything?" She'd come in the pantry where no one could see us and that's where I had my first kiss.

As I think about it, 'taking out the garbage' years later doesn't seem to have the same pleasure!

One of the favorite things that the boys liked to do was to help to butcher the pigs. This was done in the cold weather. We were fascinated with the way everything was cut up.

Hams were hung in the smoke house to cure. The skin was cut up and cooked and pressed into cakes called cracklings. We were supposed to feed them to the chickens, but it tasted so good and we ate a lot of it ourselves. That was like a treat to us. We also made sausage and scrapple. We ate good after we butchered a couple of pigs.

We also helped to catch the chickens, which would be our Sunday meal. There were so many interesting things you learned about living in the country. Today you go to the supermarket and buy all your food in packages. You never get to see how it was processed.

Our favorite animals on the farm were our horses. They were big draft horses. They could do heavy work on the farm. They were gentle animals and we loved to feed them and give them their drink at the watering trough.

Storing the hay in the barn was another chore we enjoyed.

We would jump from the hayloft and have lots of fun even though it was hard work.

In May of 1943, I graduated from Kutztown High School. I joined the U.S. Markine Corps in February of 1944. This certainly was a different life! I look back on my years at Topton with great fondness. I have many lifetime friends in my big 'family.'

A Gift of Love

Nobody here but us chickens...

A prize-winner!

Did you ever wonder how they got the apples off the top branches in the old days?

Well, now you know!

Haying time, July 1925

"Hurry up, mister, we want to go swimming!"

Hm. Notice anything unusual in the girls' photo?

(Hint: he's third from the left in the boys' photo!)

Robert Vansicle (1955-1964)

My mother died when I was six and my father remarried. I lived with an aunt and uncle in Belvedere, NJ until I was nine. Rev. Reinert had been the pastor in a church in Phillipsburg and my mother had been on the choir. My dad knew him, so made arrangements for my admission.

I remember there were always enough kids to play basketball or softball.

MAIN BUILDING LIFE

When I lived in the Main Building, we had to clean our own area and help with chores, like unloading trucks when they came, working in the kitchen, etc. I remember working the potato peeler machine. We had to peel 2-1/2 boilers of potatoes before school. We also had a potato masher... licking the beaters was a meal!

Mrs. Reinert would be in and out of the kitchen, making up the menus. I remember a big paper with the entire month's meals. Sunday dinner was always excellent: roast beef with the trimmings. There were always 'sweets and sours' at the end of the table. The dinner was prepared in the main kitchen and the boys took around the hot food to the cottages. Each cottage had an open dining room.

Mrs. Reinert ran the office. There wasn't anything she couldn't do...a real 'Renaissance woman.' Rev. Reinert had a very commanding presence. He signed all our report cards. If one person messed up, everybody suffered. We didn't like group punishment, but we learned from it.

There were morning and evening services. They weren't long. Mrs. Reinert would play, Rev. Reinert would lead. Kids would pick the scripture and a hymn. My favorites were: "Eternal Father" and "A Mighty Fortress." We also had flannelgraphs, Bible drills and the 'Good News Club.'

SOCIETY DAYS

On Tuesday, Wednesday or Thursday, you'd hear the call: "Tour coming!" These were the women from one of the congregations. They got a talk and a tour, then they got luncheon. It was always the same luncheon, so no one would say that someone else got special treatment. They were served hot dogs, filling, pepper cabbage and lemon meringue pie for dessert. We got leftovers the next day.

As a fund-raiser, we'd go to a congregation and get "auctioned off" to a family for dinner and afternoon. Many of us struck up friendships and went on vacation with that family. One kid got adopted.

COTTAGE LIFE

When I got older, I lived in the boys cottage. Robert and Mildred Fisher came and were our houseparents. He was a lineman and could do ANYTHING; carpentry, plumbing, etc. She was super with us. We grew to love them just like they were our own parents.

They had two of their own boys who lived there. Their family had a private living room, office and two bedrooms. It was a 24-hours/day, seven-day-a-week job.

They made a big difference in our lives. Before they came, we never had enough underwear or socks. They'd make sure we'd get eggs sometimes, so we didn't have to have cereal every day. We had a 'duty roster' for our chores: dishes, table, sweep porch, mop dorms, hallways, take out trash.

We learned the responsibility of making arrangements for our chores if we were away. They would give up their TV on Friday evenings to help us with homework.

"Pop" (Robert Fisher) took us camping every year at Hickory Run State Park in the Poconos. We went in the third week of June in the "Blue Beetle."

This was a bus; taking a trip in it was a religious experience. **We all prayed we'd get there!** To get all of our equipment in, we'd take out the seats in the back half. You can picture what THAT looked like! Everyone had their assigned responsibilities: two in charge of cooking, one boy had responsibility of keeping the campfire burning, etc.

We had free time on weekends. We put our name on a big blackboard under: ballfield, woods, swings, trails. Sometimes you could go downtown to the movies. We also saw the Reading Indians and heard the Lafayette Glee Club.

HARVEST HOME

The churches brought food by the truckload and carload. There were canned goods, fresh vegetables and all kinds of fruits. The boys would carry it all inside. There was a huge canning and freezing operation; canned peaches, tomatoes and a lot of other things that would last through the winter.

DOWN ON THE FARM

The Home had two farms and two farmers. We worked with them. We had a dairy herd and the raw milk was taken to be pasteurized. There were three tractors; <u>I wanted to drive a tractor so bad my teeth hurt</u>! Finally, during potato-picking season, Benjy, the maintenance man, let me drive a tractor with the potato wagon on the back. I was in Heaven! Then it came time to bring the load back to the barn.

Benjy said, "Back the tractor in." Well, I didn't want to remind him that this was the first time I'd driven a tractor FRONTWARDS and had never backed ANYTHING up! *You can already guess what happened.* I backed directly into the big barn door and knocked it off its hinges!

Benjy just looked at the mess and said, "Well, I've been wanting to get a new door for a long time. Now we will."

You could have your own garden. They'd sell you seeds at cost, then buy the produce from you when it was ripe. I had a HUGE truck patch and liked it.

THE PLAYS

Anniversary Day was the "big play." I was Johnny Appleseed (seems like 100 times) and was also in The Emperor's Nightingale, Hansel & Gretel, H.M.S. Pinafore and many more.

Little kids got to be dewdrops, squirrels and trees. (If you couldn't remember your lines, you wore brown pants and stuck your face through the hold in the tree.) Your instructions were: Point your feet towards the audience; enunciate clearly." It was nice that everyone got to take part in the plays because it made it a real 'team effort.'

The Christmas play was presented on Christmas Eve. I remember doing most of the bigger parts (shepherds, wise men, rabbis) and can still remember the lines.

One time, we all got the giggles. We were in procession with candles. Our beards were flapping. Someone looked out at the audience and whispered, "You people are lucky we're letting you go home!" It was so hilarious, it broke us up! (I guess you had to be there...)

MANY MEMORIES

We had a dam, stocked with fish. In the winter, we went ice skating. I remember how good the hot cocoa tasted.

We never went hungry...and the food was good!

I remember Miss Belser and the famous "bowl haircuts." As a matter of fact, I learned how to cut hair. There was a barber chair in the basement.

Kids had a purpose when they came out. The Home would pay your college tuition and you paid it back "when you could."

After High School, I just couldn't wait to get out to the big world. However, I missed being there a lot, because the Home was truly my home as a child.

Apple Blossom Beauty!

**Look over here...
perfect!**

Hurray! It's Springtime!

An altogether lovely portrait

Who wants to sled down with me?
Let's race!

A Gift of Love

Wonder what's so interesting off to the right?
And did you notice that today's haircuts are
EXACTLY like these? (Right back in style again!)

Having fun at the Turkey Barbeque stand!

(from left) Mr. & Mrs. Clayton George (Miriam Huber: former matron in the girls' cottage) Kenneth Boldt; Marian (Mrs. Carlton) Heckman

Catherine Falk Zenz
(1925-1935)

I remember that, when there was snow, Mrs. Henry would always insist that we wear galoshes when we walked down and back to Junior High School. I was embarrassed, because they were so big and clunky. I used to take them off and hide them under the last pine tree to the left of the bottom of the steps. I never did get caught!

When I was 13, Helen Silfies (cook) burned her leg and couldn't work for a while. I learned how to skin and fry liver (lots of it.)

Marian Heckman started working here 1937. She was only 21, but Mrs. Henry said, "We'll try you." She stayed 16 years, said: "I fooled her. I married her son!" Karl Henry died nine years later from cancer.

In 1964, she married Carlton Heckman, who was on the Board in the '40s. He served on the Board for about 8 years and was Chairman of the Admissions Committee.

I stayed 16-1/2 yrs. caring for 24 girls. Winter was the worst time. We had to get everyone in long snowsuits, boots and gloves. I used to pin the gloves on the sleeves so they wouldn't lose them all the time.

In the dining room, we had six little white tables. In the summer, we had flowers on each table. In the winter, I had a little bowl of little golden guppies on every table. Oh, the kids had a time when their fish had babies. We had a nice record player and two canaries, too. It was pretty.

The girls slept in four big rooms. There were six beds in a room. They were cute, low little beds and they each had a doll on their bed. Pastor Henry gave us two cats, "Whiskers" and "Sneekey." The children loved when the cats would curl up and purr at the bottom of their beds.

For breakfast, we'd make cold cereal and cocoa ourselves. Two girls from the main building brought over hot cereal and a hot drink. They had metal containers that fit together, with carrying handles.

Mrs. Kline and I would take turns washing the dishes and about three little girls would dry them. We'd wipe the tables, then put the clean dishes back on the tables.

Then we had worship in the morning. There was a piano in the playroom. We'd sing "Jesus Loves Me" and others from the little children's red book, then offer a prayer. When we prayed the Lord's Prayer, one of the little girls said, "Thank you for the jelly bread." It was cute.

SCHOOL DAYS

When they would get ready for school, there weren't slacks in those days. They wore starched little dresses and little pants. Friends or relatives would give dresses. Congregations also donated old dresses. The girls had a lot of dresses. We had to starch and press them. I combed all the little girls' hair and put ribbons in. They looked pretty to go to school.

While they were gone, we had to clean the house. We washed everything but the sheets and towels, which were done in the Home's laundry. We had a wash line outside. You should have seen how that looked, with all the little socks and pants hanging up, waving in the breeze.

The teacher usually came over to fetch them in the morning. At recess, they all came home and got a glass of milk, sometimes an apple and a carrot, too. At lunchtime, they brought us our dinner from the main building kitchen.

The people who worked in the main building ate in the dining room there. After the kids were 11, they lived in the main building. The boys on the east side, girls on the west side. They had a lot of beds in the bedrooms upstairs and on the third floor. It was strictly handled, but, of course, they got together sometimes.

I loved to take my girls on walks. Sometimes we'd go downtown, but soon enough, they would start to say, "Oh Miss Kaufman, let's go home." Or we'd go to the fields where the Luther Haven cottages are now. We would watch the sun set down there.

And in the summer, I would take them to the swimming pool. It was painted aqua. Our time was from 1 p.m. to 2 p.m. I had these 24 little kids, and none of them ever drowned for me.

Beyond the swimming pool was a really nice path, nice and wide. A little stream crossed that. The little kids used to love to cross on the stepping stones. There was a birch tree just past the stream. You could break little pieces of it and eat birch bark.

When the kids came home from school, they usually got a glass of milk. The Home had its own herd of cows. Some of the older kids (with a manager) would milk the cows and bring us a big container of milk. At first, they didn't have it pasteurized and it was real creamy on top. We stirred it up. But there were hunks of cream and the kids didn't like that. But they had to drink it. **I loved it!**

There was no TV to watch after school. They played outside when they came home from school. We had a sliding board with a climber, two see-saws, two nice big swings with chains. There was a playhouse with a sandbox. They would hang up things and have a good time in their 'pretend' house.

Out in back was a flower garden with paths. You could walk around through it. There was every flower you could think of. The boys tended that. They took turns. They did most of the manual labor, like mowing grass and working in the fields, picking potatoes.

Girls had to help in the house and do their part of the cleaning. When they were older, some worked in the laundry. They had to do everything the staff has to do now.

I was here under both Rev. Henry and Rev. Reinert. Mrs. Reinert was a bit more modern. We all went to church over where the Putz is. That was the chapel. The little girls all sat up front on the left hand side. The little boys sat up on the other side.

We had those pretty windows in the church. We had a real nice choir and Mrs. Henry had charge of the choir. So did Mrs. Reinert when she came. Mrs. Reinert surely was a good organist!

Christmas was really something. You see, all the children were allowed to look at the Putz. They were allowed to play with those things that were in the yard. They weren't allowed to move the trains, but there were other things you could move, like the tree with the monkey going up. They were allowed to play with things. Every year, Mrs. Henry bought or made something new for the Putz. It was really something to see!

REV. HENRY

As a young man, Henry was pastor of Trinity Lutheran Church in Topton. There was a vacancy here when the

previous Superintendent left. Dr. Henry filled in temporarily. The story he told was, that he was driving his horse
and carriage along the road.

A little girl was walking along and he said, "Are you from
the Home?" She said she was, so he brought her up the hill.
On the way, she said to Dr. Henry, "Won't you come up and
be our daddy?" That clinched it for him. He decided to
resign as pastor and took the position here.

Dr. Henry managed the farm himself. He had farmers,
but he was the manager. They had steer and a man who
took care of the chickens. They didn't have half the people
here that they do now. If he would lose his temper or something, it was no wonder. He had too much that he was
taking care of. Dr. Henry had charge of the farm, everything. It was too hard for one person.

The Henrys lived in the main building, upstairs. They
had private bedrooms. The three boys, Karl, Leonard and
Paul slept in one big room. Then Karl told me that when
someone got sick, his mother would bring that person in
their bedroom. They invited a lot of people to dine in their
dining room. It had a big oval dining table.

ANNIVERSARY DAYS

There used to be a lot of trains that would come. Many
more people attended back then, I remember. There was a
big pavillion where they sat on benches. They had a nice
stage there. All the staff had to help dress all those little
children in costume for the plays they put in.

It was something. Women from the different congregations came and sewed Tuesday, Wednesday and Thursday
of Anniversary Day. Sometimes there were three groups on
a day. They would bring all the little kids a bag of candy.
They liked to do it. Mrs. Henry wrote all those programs.
And they were good.

SOCIETY DAY

After Anniversary Day, a lot of groups would come out. It
was called Society Day. People from different churches did
mending and made whatever new things were needed. Mrs.

Henry and Mrs. Reinert took these people all around the cottages. They would come and visit us. They would look all around the cottages, upstairs and down.

They worked in the morning, then had lunch. It was always the same lunch for everyone: potato filling, hot dogs and lemon meringue pie for dessert. After lunch, they would have a program and go around to see the cottages.

HARVEST HOME

Some congregations came during the harvest season. People would come and help to can goods, make jelly, etc. You're not allowed to do that anymore.

I married Rev. Karl Henry. He was Secretary of Survey and Research of the United Lutheran Church. He had to go to every state and visit the Mission Churches, and to pick places to build Mission Churches.

CRAFT PROGRAM

Mrs. Carlton L. Heckman with craft group.

Rev. Reinert asked me to come back, but they didn't have children then to take care of. They asked me to do the craft program. I liked that. I went one day a week to the Annie Lowry house. We had crafts in the living room. Before then, they just sat and didn't do anything. The old folks didn't like it when Carlton married me, because they liked the things I would plan.

Every day I went to a different group. Each Wednesday, I went to the Caum Home in Reading. The women would be sitting at five card tables, waiting for me. They would say, "You're just like the mail man...you come through all kinds of weather!" I even went in the snow, so I wouldn't disappoint them.

At noon, I would eat with them in that beautiful white dining room and thought I was eating at the White House!

This era of The Lutheran Home is "history." It's quiet now on campus. There are no kids yelling and running around, playing games, skipping rope.

There's no more school. No lessons, no homework to complain about and do anyway.

There is no more yodeling, no sneaking into town for forbidden sweets or making plans to meet Stubby for some baked goods.

These children from another time, now known as the Lutheran Home Alumni Association, meet here annually over the Memorial Day holiday. Sadly, fewer come back each year. We would hope that an effort could be made, in this electronic age, to capture many more memories from these special folks very soon, so it all does not fade away.

If that could be done, perhaps they could be included in the update of this book, scheduled for 25 years from now!

The cottages where the orphans lived have been recycled, as has the main building. Where the orphans lived and grew up, there are now serious adults in offices, doing work and having meetings.

All these young children smiling at you in these photos have grown, traveled, achieved and have children and grandchildren of their own. The years have taken their toll. Some are buried on foreign soil, some close to home.

The mission has changed, enlarged, broadened in wondrous ways, far past anything the founders could probably have imagined. We reach over 6,000 people every day in five counties in eastern Pennsylvania, regardless of race, creed or ethnic origin.

The second hundred years starts now.

Chapter 10

THAT'S ENTERTAINMENT!

Mrs. Ida Lisette Seffing Henry was surely the "Cecil B. DeMille" of The Lutheran Home at Topton. Under her direction, almost every production seemed to have "a cast of thousands!" Seriously, EVERY-ONE was in the show...every show! Every child, staffer and employee was in show business!

If she wanted to learn how to do something 'new and different,' she merely got on the train at Topton station and went to New York City's Radio City Music Hall. She'd take her secret weapon...some of her homemade caramels (see recipe) and talk directly with the Stage Manager. She'd outline her challenge and, on the spot, she'd get the best sources, addresses and tips! This is the secret of how The Lutheran Home at Topton could come up with some as-tounding special effects!

For instance, she'd decided to produce an epic on the Israelites in Egypt, including building the pyramids, slaves, Pharaohs, the plagues and the escape from Egypt. Her only problem...she wasn't happy with the parting of the Red Sea. It didn't look right.

From her Radio City Music Hall contacts, she learned about 'water cloth.' Several long pieces of thin, silk multi-color cloth were waved from their ends, simulating the sea. In the middle of the sea, there were boys under the water cloth, facing the inside edges.

After Moses commanded the sea to part, the boys crouch-ing under the undulating cloth moved the center pieces away from each other so the Israelites could pass through "on dry land." The rest of the water quieted down.

Then, when Pharaoh's chariots came rushing up, the water would get very rough as the water cloth was waved violently. The boys on each side of the center path would rise up, run together and all the Egyptians would be 'drowned!' A very effective finale to a monumental epic. (*Now, don't tell anyone the secret!*)

The productions were first-class. You can see for yourself that the costumes and props were well-done and imaginative. No, these were not long-running productions...though they were repeated year after year. The great fun was that EVERYONE was involved. True, the older kids got the main roles, but there were parts for little flowers, trees, etc.

Unfortunately for us, these fine productions took place long before camcorders and videotape. If you were fortunate enough to be in the plays or the audience, see if these pictures bring back some memories of a golden age so many years ago. Share the memories! We who have only cracked and faded photographs are envious of your experiences!

P.S. We've mentioned before that when Mrs. Henry went to Radio City Music Hall to get first-class staging information, she took along her home made caramels. Well, her granddaughter, Nancy Henry Kline, gave us the recipe!

Mrs. Ida Henry's Caramel Recipe

. 4 squares unsweetened baking chocolate

. 1 cup dark Karo

. 2 cups dark brown sugar

. 1 cup milk

Put in heavy bottom kettle, bring to boil,

keep stirring on low heat

After 1/2 hour, add:

. 1/4 lb. butter, Keep stirring 10-20 minutes

Test in ice water for hard ball; pour into buttered pans.

Scenes from the "Moses" pageant: Moses in the bulrushes; Israelite slaves in Egypt; Moses parts the Red Sea

A Gift of Love

The Egyptian soldiers
and charioteers pursue
the Israelites. Look at
the detail on the horses!

Moses receives the ten
commandments.
He comes down from
Mt. Sinai.

Palm Dancers from the Moses Pageant

A desert oasis...complete with tent, palm trees and sheep!

Here comes the circus! Perhaps you wondered how they got the weightlifter on a real elephant, hm? Isn't that a fantastic costume? We also have oriental performers and a festively outfitted circus band!

C'mon out west and meet these fearsome gunslingers, Indian braves and squaws, hard-ridin' and ropin' cowboys... all of them part of the show, everybody's having a ball!

Flowers in
Solomon's
Garden

Elijah
fed by
the ravens

Yahveh
is stronger
than Baal

Well, hi cutie!

A Gift of Love

Lots of everyone's favorite fairy tales...

There you have a just a bit of the 'flavor' of the astounding variety of shows, pageants and presentations which Mrs. Ida Henry dreamed up and then brought to life. Remember that EVERY child and employee had a part in these plays and presentations!

For me, poring over the boxes and boxes of old photos has truly been 'time travel.' I will peer into a young face and feel those eyes looking back at me.

The only hard part is putting all the rest of them back...unused. They have the musty smell of great age upon them. Some are cracked, many have cryptic notes on their back: "3 col. bot. left." "Feature lead." I know that there are many precious scrapbooks which contain the original news-paper stories.

I will leave you with two of my favorite photos. I showed this one above, with its gaggle of gigglers, to the Alumni attending the annual meeting on May 29, 1995. There was just as much laughter then! Seems the girls were just taking a soda break when the photographer saw a 'photo op.' He got them a little closer together, but they were just having fun and really didn't pay much attention. They live forever now, young and healthy, laughing in the summer sunshine. Perhaps someday we might trace the lives...or perhaps we should just smile and let the memory be its own reward.

Here are the Natter twins. They were born Nov. 8, 1937 and have been written up in many publications.

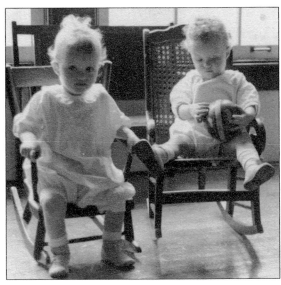

Martin & Luther Natter

They are just one of several sets of twins who spent their childhood years at The Lutheran Home. You can see that there are many more stories to be told.

This part of this volume will be YOUR look back into the lives of those who spent their childhood at this remarkable place. Do look at them from time to time.

They have spent too many years in dark and musty boxes. Like all of us, they **do** love the light.

Afterword

The second century at The Lutheran Home at Topton begins with TWO new leaders.

The Rev. Daun E. McKee, Ph.D., has been named President and Chief Executive Officer.

Mitchell G. Possinger is the new Chairman of the Board.

Actually, this volume is going to press just as these gentlemen are taking over their positions, so we wish them all the best.

Is it a coincidence that the last page of this history of the <u>first</u> hundred years introduces the two men with the toughest responsibilities for starting the <u>second</u> hundred years?

Doubtful.

As you have seen in these pages, this institution has felt the hand of God at all times, beginning even before there was anything but dreams.

Nothing has changed.

The Rev. Daun E. McKee, Ph.D.
President and
Chief Executive Officer

Mitchell G. Possinger
Chairman of the Board

APPENDIX

Board of Trustees

Name	Parish	Years
47. Mr. Wayne R. Bardman	Sumneytown Parish	1941-1947
48. Mr. Harry S. Miller	Zionsville Parish	1941-1952
49. Mr. John K. Messner	Muddy Creek Parish	1941-1943
50. Dr. Edwin D. Funk, M.D.	Atonement, Wyomissing	1941-1966
51. Rev. C. Elwood Huegel	St. Paul, Orwigsburg	1942-1952
52. Rev. Carlton L. Heckman	Trinity, Kutztown	1942-1950
53. Mr. Edwin E. Wisser, Sr.	Grace, Allentown	1943-1948
54. Rev. Mark K. Trexler	Calvary, Laureldale	1946-1952
55. Mr. Harold M. Weishaupt	Holy Trinity, Hershey	1947-1956
56. Mr. M.D. Walborn	Trinity, Pottsville	1947-1963
57. Mr. Richard T. Williams	Trinity, Reading	1948-1969
58. Rev. Elton L. Angstadt	Sumneytown Parish	1949-1964
59. Rev. Elmer F. Weinrich	Blandon-Shoemakersville	1950-1953
60. Rev. Raymond J. Heckman	St. James, Allentown	1950-1969
61. Rev. Paul J. Dundore	Amityville	1951-1964
62. Rev. Victor Kroninger	Grace, Shillington	1951-1968
63. Rev. Clarence A. Steigerwalt	Freidensburg Parish	1952-1965
64. Rev. J. W. Bittner	St. John, Kutztown	1952-1964
65. Rev. Elmer R. Deibert	St. Mark, Reading	1952-1961
66. Mr. George Grimes	St. John, Reading	1952-1958
67. Mr. Charles Emhardt	St. John, Hamburg	1952-1970
68. Mr. Claude Yost	Christ, Allentown	1952-1958
69. Rev. Rufus E. Kern, D.D.	Topton Parish	1953-1965
70. Mr. Clarence S. Dietrich	Kutztown Parish	1955-1967
71. Mr. William F. Wolfe, Jr.	Grace, Royersford	1956-1976
72. Mr. Harry J. Becker	St. John, Reading	1958-1991
73. Mr. Harold C. Barette	St. Luke, Allentown	1958-1971
74. Rev. Paul J. Henry, D.D.	Trinity, Robesonia	1961-1977
75. Mr. Harold Aulenbach	Wyomissing Hills	1962-1969
76. Rev. Samuel C. Jaxheimer	St. Luke, Reading	1962-1977
77. Mr. Effenger M. Erb	St. John, Boyertown	1962-1968
78. Mr. Lester E. Ost	Trinity, Pottsville	1963-1969
79. Rev. Robert H. Loucks	Trinity, Topton	1964-1965
80. Rev. Richard O. Scherch	St. Mark's, Birdsboro	1964-1965
81. Rev. William A. Fluck	Center Square	1964-1979
82. Rev Frank Radcliffe, D.D.	Holy Spirit, Reading	1965-1980
83. Rev. Paul H. Spohn	Grimsville Parish	1965-1966
84. Rev. William Marburger	Orwigsburg	1965-1980
85. Rev. Alfred L. Long	St. John, Nazareth	1965-1981
86. Rev. William A. Davis	St. John, Kutztown	1966-1968
87. Dr. Clyde Kelchner	Allentown Parish	1966-1984
88. Rev. Larry Schell	St. Paul, Amityville	1968-1979
89. Mr. Samuel W. Weiss	St. John, Boyertown	1968-1978
90. Rev. Martin Zirkle	St. Michael, Hamburg	1968-1976
91. Rev. Charles Kern	Cedar, Cetronia	1969-1976
92. Dr. Lawrence Reimert	Union, Neffs	1969-1981
93. Mr. J. Park Smith	Topton Parish	1970-1978
94. Mr. William Yoder	Kutztown Parish	1970-1982
95. Rev. Elton P. Richards, Jr.	Reading Parish	1970-1978
96. Fred Ruccius	Reading Parish	1971-1978

Board of Trustees

Name	Parish	Years
146. Mr. Daniel G. Ebbert*	Sinking Spring Parish	1988-
147. Rev. Philip S. Bendle, III	Trinity, Pottsville	1989-
148. Rev. Wayne R. Kaufman	Trinity, Bechtelsville	1989-
149. Rev. Richard L. Krapf	St. Mark, Birdsboro	1989-
150. Rev. Paul L. Schoffstall	Nativity, Allentown	1989-1992
151. Rev. Donald W. Hayn	Shepherd of the Hills, Egypt	1990-1993
152. Mr. George M. Gebhardt	Trinity, Pottsville	1990-
153. Mr. Ezekiel Ketchum	Trinity, Reading	1990-
154. Dr. Jonathan Messerli	Allentown Parish	1991-1992
155. Mr. R. Keith Broome	St. Paul, Fleetwood	1991-
156. Rev. Robert R. Mitchell	Christ, Spangsville	1991-
157. Rev. Cheryl F. Meinschein	Bethany, Stony Creek Mills	1991-1993
158. Mrs. Mildred March	St. John, Boyertown	1992-
159. Mrs. Nadine Oswald	Christ, Schuylkill Haven	1992-
160. Mr. Mitchell Possinger	Union, Neffs	1992-
161. Mr. William Angstadt	Trinity, Reading	1992-
162. Mr. Robert E. Gehman	Alsace, Reading	1992-
163. Mrs. Judith E. Stoudt	Atonement, Wyomissing	1992-
164. Mr. James R. Fegley, Esq.	Reformation, Reiffton	1993-
165. Rev. James H. Wolford	St. John, Allentown	1993-
166. Rev. Jack W. Murphy	Frieden, Hegins	1993-
167. Mrs. Kathryn Pelgrift Taylor		1993-
168. Rev. Richard H. Schaefer	Calvary, Laureldale	1993-
169. Rev. Luther H. Routté	Atonement, Wyomissing	1994-
170. Mrs. Susan E. Wambaugh		1994-

* = Chairperson

TOPTON ORPHANS' HOME SONG

Oh! Orphans' Home at Topton,
With joy we sing to thee,
We love to come from far and near
To greet our Home so dear.
'Tis here, - where God Almighty
Through His bride, the church doth heed
The cry of Orphan children,
And supplies their every need.

CHORUS

Oh! Orphans' Home at Topton;
For thee, our prayers ascend,
To thee, our toils and cares be given,
Till toils and cares shall end.

We love thy flowery meadows,
Thy paths through shady woods,
Thy orchards with their bounteous store
Of fragrant, luscious fruit.
Thy bubbling springs and streamlets,
Green fields and mountain air,
Our gracious God hath blessed thee
With beauty everywhere.

ALUMNI ASSOCIATION MEMBERS

1. Sallie Elizabeth Carl
2. Clair Eugene Carl
3. Emma Rebecca Shenfelder
4. Ralph Saylor Shenfelder
5. Walter Madenford
6. Virdie Madenford
7. Elizabeth A. Greenwood
8. Eva M. Greenwood
9. Katie S. Tureck
10. Samuel J. Tureck
11. William W. Tolbert
12. Carl R. Smith
13. Alice Kathleen Kennedy
14. Anna Smith
15. Morris Smith
16. Eleanora E. Boxmeyer
17. Mira May Saylor
18. Howard Wortz
19. Edna Wortz
20. Paul A. Eben
21. LeRoy F. Eben
22. Ada M. Bixler
23. Florence E. Bixler
24. Margaret E. Aaron
25. John D. Aaron
26. Ella Meyner
27. Louisa Meyner
28. Emma Meyner
29. Robert D. Werley
30. John I. Weiser
31. Mary S. Fidler
32. Charles A. Fidler
33. Carl A. Fleisher
34. Lillian O. Fleisher
35. Charles S. Seeman
36. Russell E. Seeman
37. Florence E. Westney
38. Hazel D. Westney
39. Harry E. Westney
40. Lenora W. C. Kannaple
41. Harry J. Steltz
42. William E. Steltz
43. George C. W. Brueningsen
44. Harry H. Rice
45. Anna Jacobs
46. Ralph Kemmerle
47. Florence Kemmerle
48. Anna Cervinka
49. Helen Conrad
50. Elda Conrad
51. Pearl Laura Koppenheffer
52. Ralph Allen Koppenheffer
53. Maude Jennie Kauffmen
54. William F. Kauffmen
55. Andrew McKinley Bock
56. Evelyn Dienstel
57. Laura Dienstel
58. Laura Elizabeth Rudloff
59. Henry George Rudloff
60. Rosa Maria Wagner
61. Ida Kathryn Wagner
62. Raymond S. George
63. Christopher Carl Haas
64. Blanche Augusta Forner
65. Esther Reinbold
66. Charles Samuel Engle
67. Arthur Edwin Engle
68. Edgar Shay Mathers
69. Lottie A. Hahn
70. Mary McKnight
71. David McKnight
72. Blanche McShane
73. Herbert McShane
74. Harold Franklin Brinker
75. Harvey Luther Carpenter
76. Emma Margaret Bachman
77. Joseph Emory White
78. Calvin Franklin Blose
79. William Carl Falkenstein
80. Agnes Hildebrandt
81. Charles Harold Hissner
82. Frank Bishop

83.	John Platt	129.	Florence Irene Conard
84.	Walter Frank Platt	130.	Samuel M. Conard
85.	Laura Kudel	131.	Susan C. Conard
86.	Leonard John Fogley	132.	Roy Earl Lauck
87.	Russell Lee Fogley	133.	Earl Henry Gable
88.	Cora M. Stettler	134.	Bertha Lillian Schappel
89.	Edna M. Stettler	135.	Lafayette Hay Schappel
90.	Lena Roselda Wary	136.	Thomas Hay Schappel
91.	Carrie Alma Wary	137.	Thomas Emanuel Siegfried
92.	Robert Henry Platt	138.	Catharine Vincent Siegfried
93.	James Israel Ruppert	139.	Edna Ruth Billiard
94.	Earl Abraham Ruppert	140.	Violet Catharine Billiard
95.	Emma Marie Brossman	141.	Louisa Eckert
96.	Charles Ezra Brossman	142.	Frederick Lewis Eckert
97.	Theodore Albert Sherman	143.	Harry Herman Eckert
98.	Jacob John Sherman	144.	Esther Sybilla Lengle
99.	Laura Frances Forner	145.	Martha Elizabeth Long
100.	Robert Russell Spangler	146.	Evelyn Elizabeth Long
101.	Caleb Weidner	147.	George Milton Long
102.	Floyd Harry Blose	148.	Norman J. Bortz
103.	Bertha May Kohman	149.	Warren George Bortz
104.	Truman Henry Ettwein	150.	John Hoelzel
105.	Ethel Marion Ettwein	151.	Edna Estella Ruffner
106.	Bessie Gertrude Young	152.	Elenora Ruffner
107.	Lewis Howard Young	153.	Pauline Heckman
108.	John Thomas Kolp	154.	Walter F. Allender
109.	Evelyn B. Lavenburg	155.	Helen DeThample
110.	Charles D. H. Durn	156.	Claude Herbert Witman
111.	Walter Elmer Underkoffler	157.	Mabel Rowe
112.	Edward Elmer Underkoffler	158.	Paul Gerhart Grimes
113.	Florence Arlene Crossly	159.	Henry Posey Grimes
114.	William Allen Drake	160.	Mary Ada Waldman
115.	Clarence Leroy Drake	161.	Charles George Waldman
116.	Charles Henry Steibing	162.	Mary E. Walter
117.	Minnie May Kinderman	163.	Melvin G. Walter
118.	Henry William Kinderman	164.	Howard M. Adolph
119.	Raymond Lewis Smith	165.	John Abraham Adolph
120.	Horace Pysher	166.	George Fradeneck
121.	Marshall Pysher	167.	Esther Rebecca Fradeneck
122.	Dorothy Elizabeth Steibing	168.	John Jacob Weidner
123.	Luther Buehler	169.	Leroy M. Weidner
124.	Stanly Buehler	170.	Henry Short Dolan
125.	Leon Buehler	171.	Mary Elizabeth Dolan
126.	Edwin Moyer	172.	James Edward Dolan
127.	Esta Moyer	173.	Catharine Milander
128.	Abner Moyer	174.	Julia Susan Milander

175. Wilson Irwin Bortz
176. Kathryn May Bortz
177. Charles Edwin Bortz
178. Marie H. Held
179. Willard Pannebecker
180. Donald Pannebecker
181. Luther George Frick
182. Theodore Charles Frick
183. Benneville A. High
184. Russell J. Yeisley
185. Ellwood D. Yeisley
186. Marcus Augustus Wagner
187. Effie Naomi Wagner
188. Wilbur Charles Held
189. Arthur Leroy Held
190. Thomas E. High
191. Frederick Geschwindt
192. George Geschwindt
193. Margaret May White
194. Cecelia Elizabeth White
195. Vincent Francis White
196. Irvin Thomas Miller
197. George Gendricks
198. Mary Tryphena Radel
199. Ada Gabriella
200. Emma Jane Perschau
201. Godfried Rudolph Perschau
202. John David Perschau
203. Robert Theodore Perschau
204. Paul Christian Gilham
205. Clarence Miller Gilham
206. William Edelman
207. Catharine Pannebecker
208. Helen Pannebecker
209. Larue S. Ruppert
210. Helen S Ruppert
211. Earl Benjamin Trexler
212. John Samuel Pauley
213. Howard Boyer
214. Raymond H Forrey
215. Chester H. Forrey
216. Daniel H. Forrey
217. Carl Horn
218. Arthur B. Moyer
219. Michael Vodilla
220. Jacob Vodilla

221. Kathryn Elizabeth Fields
222. Mary Elizabeth Fields
223. Olivia Kathryn Dorward
224. Jonathan A. Dorward
225. Theodore Ressler Unverzagt
226. Christine W. Unverzagt
227. Earl J. F. Huver
228. Helen A. Huver
229. Herman R. Unverzagt
230. Arthur A. Unverzagt
231. Mary E. Dietrich
232. Alice Rebecca Dietrich
233. John William Dietrich
234. Herman Kresch
235. Theodore Seiberling
236. Wilbur James Bunn
237. Charles Harvey Bunn
238. Neomia L. Spangler
239. Clarence H. Spangler
240. Harry Edward Reichard
241. Lewis Christian Frank
242. Paul C. Frank
243. Edward Frederick Filbert
244. Paul Moyer Filbert
245. William Frederick Filbert
246. Kathryn Emily Filbert
247. Myrtle E. Huey
248. William O. Huey
249. Charles Ephraim Huey
250. Walter Herman Hertzog
251. Martin Luther Hertzog
252. Charles Paul Hess
253. Caroline Mock
254. Miriam Kathryn Uhler
255. Alma Uhler
256. Lillian Rebecca Weaver
257. Florence Dorothy Weaver
258. Mildred Bitler
259. Anna Helen Bitler
260. Celesta Regine Kleintop
261. Viola Estella Kleintop
262. Bertha Trexler
263. Raymond Smith Behm
264. George Albert Grabey
265. Dorothy May Rohrbach
266. Helen Margaret Rohrbach

267. Elvin Russel Hartman
268. Daniel Wesley Hartman
269. Frederick Morgan Smith
270. Eva Hummel
271. Florence K. M. Reiff
272. Emily A. R. Reiff
273. Tilmus Hummel
274. John Woodrow Eppinger
275. Howard Elbert Eppinger
276. Thomas Raymond Boone
277. Elizabeth Louisa Boone
278. Emma Elizabeth Wagner
279. Charles Henry Wagner
280. George Hayward Eppinger
281. Jacob Elwood Leed
282. Mary Elizabeth Leed
283. Irene Viola Fegley
284. Elsie May Fegley
285. Loretta Bechtel
286. Paul Edward Druckenmiller
287. William Claude Peters
288. Hazel Mary Eppinger
289. Willard Lester Fehnel
290. Sylvester Russel Fehnel
291. Evelyn Esther Roth
292. Louis Dieruff Moore
293. Maude Gertrude Kern
294. Mildred Ellen Underkoffer
295. Kenneth R. P. Wetherick
296. Raymond O. Wetherick
297. Luther Trexler Behler
298. Joseph Solomon Miller
299. Frank Yost
300. Howard Lester Noll
301. Violet Florence Noll
302. Robert Paul Wagner
303. Vera D. Redcay
304. Helen Louisa Hess
305. Jennie May Hess
306. Clyde George Rohland
307. Emma Elizabeth Rohland
308. Anna Louisa Boyer
309. Mattie May Boyer
310. Edgar Paul Painter
311. Edwin Sterling Painter
312. John Clayton Harris
313. Herbert Daniel Harris
314. Dorothy Kathryn Weidner
315. Walter Shettler Weidner
316. Henry Hoffmaster Weidner
317. Chester Earl Werst
318. Russell Henry Werst
319. Paul Leon Wertman
320. Mary Margaret Weidner
321. Charles W. Weidner
322. Sarah Jane Stobert
323. Dorothy S. A. Brown
324. Clearfield Jackson Linebar
325. Clyde Samuel Linebar
326. Doris Irene Linebar
327. John Weston Laity
328. Violet May Laity
329. Arnold Joseph Lotz
330. James Clark Lotz
331. Frederick Perry Gruhler
332. Anna Mary Gruhler
333. Harold Alfred Naus
334. Paul Willard Boyer
335. Kenneth Ralph Boyer
336. Grace Esther Mullen
337. Hardee E. Mullen
338. Neomia Elva Gangloff
339. Erma May Gangloff
340. William Frederick Moll
341. Evelyn Augusta Seifert
342. Grace Margaret Seifert
343. Lyle Harold Seifert
344. Gilbert Albert Seifert
345. Eva Sarah Kulp
346. Ernest Oliver Naus
347. Viola Martha Naus
348. Grace Amelia Naus
349. John Kenneth Naus
350. Lenora Esther Smith
351. Nellie Lavina Smith
352. Harry Arthur Schylaskee
353. Marguerite Josephine Reid
354. Russel Elmer Reid
355. Dorothy Marie Rist
356. Mabel Rosanna Rist
357. Raymond Anthony Rist
358. Earl Adam Baganstose

359. Harrison Alvin Roth
360. Thomas Charles Reinhart
361. Frederick Peter Reinhart
362. Louise Alice Reinhart
363. Frederick J. Smith
364. Martha Louisa Smith
365. Catharine Smith
366. Francis Charles Smith
367. Mildred Alice Lutz
368. John William Lewis
369. Charles Wesley Lewis
370. Mary Elizabeth Fogle
371. George Richard Fogle
372. Robert Henry Drey
373. Marlowe June Drey
374. Elton Oscar Schafer
375. Frances Susannah Wise
376. Beatrice Stella Wise
377. John Roy Wise
378. Elmer Hartman
379. Margaret Elizabeth Jones
380. Marion Myrtle Jones
381. Kathryn May Kirchner
382. Henry Edwin Kerr
383. Harvey Abram Kerr
384. Emma Elizabeth Frey
385. Herman Klann
386. Thelma May Klann
387. Dorothy Marie Young
388. Jesse H. Gray, Jr.
389. William John Gray
390. Albert Samuel Gray
391. Mark Ivan Snyder
392. Raymond Hipsch
393. Elmer Franklin Burrell
394. Arline Virginia Kirchner
395. Edward Folk
396. Woodrow Wilson Kirchner
397. Albert Leroy Kirchner
398. Verna Laura Hershberger
399. Hilda Pauline Hershberger
400. Pauline Oswald
401. Josephine Oswald
402. Anna Alice Oswald
403. Kathryn R Murray
404. Ethel Geneva Murray
405. Harrison Moyer
406. Harry Moyer
407. Erwin Moyer
408. Annie Viola Moyer
409. Charles W. Laudenslager
410. Warren L. Laudenslager
411. Paul Franklin Brooks
412. Vincent Alfred Oswald
413. William Arthur Gernert
414. John Franklin Gernert
415. Mahlon Herbert Hartman
416. Russel J. Murray
417. Harry William Murray
418. Allen Wilmer Hess
419. Ellwood Thomas Hess
420. Arlene Sallie Dehrs
421. Russel Clayton Dehrs
422. Charlotte Ruth Irwin
423. Woodrow Wilson Luckey
424. Alvin Luckey
425. Donald Luckey
426. Evelyn Emma Luckey
427. Kathryn Amy Guenther
428. John James Guenther
429. Lawrence Wade Heffner
430. Mildred Carrie Kistler
431. Dorothy Alverta Batdorf
432. Millie Eneta Batdorf
433. Gordon Jeremiah Heydt
434. Harold Calvin Heydt
435. Kenneth Edwin Heydt
436. Paul Francis Heydt
437. Ernest Wellington Mattern
438. Clarence Allen Mattern
439. Kermet Rhump
440. William Rhump
441. Irwin Harold Gougler
442. Laura E. Gougler
443. Clarence Jacob Gougler
444. Emil Joseph Umberger
445. Cyrannes Edward Miller
446. Ethel Fidela Umberger
447. Ruth H. Klotz
448. Melvin F. Klotz
449. Luther Najarian
450. Ethel Mildred Finkbone

451. Virginia May Finkbone
452. Irene Beatrice Finkbone
453. Florence Arlene Stehly
454. Fred Merritt Stehly
455. Revere James Hoffman
456. Kermet Bauer Heydt
457. Lawrence W. Miller
458. Beatrice Irene Rennig
459. Dorothy Margaret Rennig
460. Lewis Henry Rennig
461. May Irene Worman
462. Anna M. Worman
463. Annie R. Wertman
464. Edward Fred Davis
465. Willard Harvey Worman
466. Orville Henry Reich
467. Mary Elizabeth Reich
468. Thomas Wilson Heck
469. Mildred Elizabeth Heck
470. Carl Willis Long
471. Chester LeRoy Long
472. Beatrice Roberta Weaver
473. Warren Reuben Lavenberg
474. Betty Florence Wolfe
475. Mildred Anna Mertz
476. William Richard Schultz
477. Edith Cordes Schultz
478. John Murphy
479. Joseph Murphy
480. Charles George Baird
481. Arthur Garrett Dieffenbach
482. Harold Dresher
483. Elizabeth Anna Baird
484. Herman Miller
485. Mary Anna Hoffman
486. Helen Elizabeth Hoffman
487. Catharine Florence Glose
488. Dorothy Irene Glose
489. Elizabeth Machajdik
490. Paul Machajdik
491. Floyd Harper Underkoffler
492. Inez Mae Underkoffler
493. Carson Miles Underkoffler
494. Wayne Austin Underkoffler
495. Willard Dalton Miller
496. Helen Violet Miller
497. George Machajdik
498. Ludmila Machajdik
499. Rolland Reiter
500. Sallie Martha Reiter
501. Gertrude Maria Miller
502. Catharine May Miller
503. John Yanchurak
504. Anna Yanchurak
505. Ethel Virginia Baum
506. Walter Oliver Derrick
507. William Edward Derrick
508. Arlene May Derrick
509. Gladys Riske
510. Shirley Jane Ruffner
511. John Schwartz Hower
512. Richard Grant Hauck
513. Harry N. Hauck
514. Elizabeth May Weikel
515. Alfred V. Scheetz
516. John Norman Baus
517. Sadie Mildred Baus
518. Jeanette Baricka
519. Francis R. Baricka
520. John Stephen Baricka
521. Ammon Morris Rabenold
522. Mark Joseph Hartzell
523. Anna Elizabeth Moyer
524. Esther Grace Moyer
525. Robert Oren Leidy
526. Betty Fern Leidy
527. Harold Boyer Sloan
528. Paul William Hess
529. Catharine Levina Elizabeth Falk
530. Howard Gilbert Lewellyn Falk
531. Edna Charlotte Rissmiller
532. Franklin William Rissmiller
533. Mary Anna Rissmiller
534. Evelin Virginia Gable Wartluft
535. Lillian Marguerite Wartluft
536. Helen Catherine Moyer
537. Ralph Edgar Snyder
538. Robert Elmer Snyder
539. Marion Verna Zacharias
540. Anna Elizabeth Benzel
541. Evan Earl Benzel
542. William Daniel Benzel

543. Paul Fehnel Silfies
544. Robert Ulysses Silfies
545. Ida Alvesta Silfies
546. Eleanor Kiefer
547. John Robert Trexler
548. Charles Henry Lewis Trexler
549. Walter John Rash
550. Amuel Rash
551. Martha Eva Rash
552. Alma Helen Rash
553. Lida Amelia Rash
554. Wilmer Raymond Moyer
555. Mary Jane Moyer
556. Eleanor Ruth Moyer
557. Lester LeRoy Hottle
558. Harvey David Hottle
559. Paul Francis German
560. William George German
561. Arthur Eugene Wieser
562. Walter Charles Wieser
563. Dorothy Marian Stehly
564. Laura May Stehly
565. Luther Cyrus Silfies
566. Lee George Grogg
567. Harold Robert Grogg
568. Esther Elizabeth Grogg
569. Grace Mae Grogg
570. Ruth Myrtle Bauer
571. Anna Freda Bauer
572. John George Bauer
573. Robert Russel Bauer
574. Mary Alice Mars
575. William Allen Mars
576. Oliver Elwood Shook
577. Edwin Kenneth Shook
578. Helen Catharine Schreiber
579. Walter Edward Schreiber
580. Virginia Mae Schreiber
581. Earl Jacob Lahr
582. Elwood Harlan Lahr
583. Woodrow Dennison Lahr
584. Robert Edward Smith
585. William Frederick Smith
586. Myrtle Irene Laudenslager
587. Charles Henry Laudenslager
588. George Edward Laudenslager

589. Lloyd Daniel Reitnauer
590. Harvey Henry Reitnauer
591. William Lawrence Reitnauer
592. Grace Gertrude Palmer
593. Ruth Elizabeth Walter
594. Kathryn Edith Walter
595. Dorothy Edna Walter
596. Calvin Elmer Laudenslager
597. Edward William Backhaus
598. George H. Derr
599. Elsie Backhaus
600. Ceclia Wilhelmina Gerber
601. John Schaeffer Sterling
602. Martin Jurek
603. John Jurek
604. Helen Jurek
605. Anna Jurek
606. Eva Pauline Laudenslager
607. Mary Smock
608. Dorothy Smock
609. William Smock
610. Marion May Fisher
611. Frances Beinlich
612. Martin Junior Clauser
613. Raymond Owen Burns
614. Beatrice June Burns
615. John Carl Gabel
616. George Donald Gabel
617. Pearl Arlene Vandegrift
618. Stella Elizabeth Vandegrift
619. Betty Kathryn Vandegrift
620. Shirley Ruth Vandegrift
621. Donald Raymond Schaeffer
622. Dorothy Gladys Eickhoff
623. Clarence Woodrow Eickhoff
624. Wallace George Eickhoff
625. Gloria May Eickhoff
626. Frances Lorraine Eickhoff
627. Earl Wilbert Snyder
628. Robert William Snyder
629. John Warren Snyder
630. Francis Frederick Boldt
631. Helen Emma Boldt
632. Pauline Elizabeth Boldt
633. Paul Luther Einsel
634. Grace Miriam Einsel

635. Francis James Bower
636. Ruth Bower
637. Marie Bower
638. Virginia Elizabeth
     Bower
639. George Frederick
     Heckendorn
640. George Franklin Klinger
641. Carl Leonhard Klinger
642. William Frederick
     Hafner
643. Harry Luther Hafner
644. John Martin Hafner
645. Kathryn Pauline Hayes
646. Bessie Belle Hayes
647. George Clyde Shurr
648. Clair Scott Shurr
649. Jacob Adam Fisher
650. George Jeremiah Fisher
651. Joann Lytle
652. Darlis Smith
653. Alfred Truman Smith
654. Doyle K. Smith
655. Burton C. Hilliard
656. Robert E. Hilliard
657. Grace Beatrice Hertzog
658. Mildred Ethel Hertzog
659. Pauline Mae Eschbach
660. Mary Frances Bauer
661. Ingeborg Elizabeth
     Bauer
662. Harry William Hoverter
663. Harrison Hoverter
664. Daniel Paul Edelman
665. Harold H. Hummer
666. Stanley H. Hummer
667. Martin H. Hummer
668. Betty Jean Kleckner
669. Jeanettte Brobst
     Kleckner
670. Ruth Mae Kleckner
671. Madeline Marie
     Kleckner
672. Anna Adeline
     Werkheiser
673. Dorothy Alma Daniels
674. Robert Harry Daniels
675. Eleanor Betty Daniels
676. Mary Elizabeth Klein
677. William Richard Klein
678. Pearl Evelyn Gum
679. Geary Amos Gum
680. John Emery Gum
681. Sarah Jeanette Lytle
682. Kenneth J. Boldt
683. Carl August Boldt
684. Elizabeth J. Boldt
685. Mae Jean Gum
686. Donald Allen Gum
687. Thomas H. Reidnauer
688. Henry H. Reidnauer
689. James Francis Neuce
690. William Tyndal Randall
691. Martha Elizabeth Randall
692. Robert Harley Randall
693. Pearl Wilhelmina Grube
694. Richard Vernon Hecker
695. Kathryn Jane Hecker
696. George Merrit Cressman
697. Evelyn Lorraine Cressman
698. Russell Howard Beck
699. Lester A. Miller
700. Leon Henry Adams
701. Dorothy Reagan
702. Beatrice Reagan
703. William Reagan, Jr.
704. Richard Paul Wilson
705. Marjorie Louise Wilson
706. Bertha Viola Ressler
707. Clayton R. Miller
708. Beatrice Warmkessel
709. Beulah Warmkessel
710. Fern Anna Eifert
711. Walter Albert Eifert
712. Paul H. Wegman
713. Irma Wegman
714. Samuel Pershing Holtry
715. Jacob Walter Holtry
716. Blanche May Holtry
717. Winifred E. Wertman
718. Vincent T. Wertman
719. Winifred R. Wertman

720. Eva H. Feger
721. Dorothy M. Feger
722. Hilda M. Feger
723. Daisy M. Feger
724. Edward Coleman
725. Imogene Coleman
726. Doris Irene Morgan
727. Howard W. Morgan
728. Robert Edwin Morgan
729. Walter Richard Frankenfield
730. Betty May Fulmer
731. Betty Jane Mummey
732. Mary Joyce Mummey
733. Emma May Mummey
734. Samuel Oliver Mummey
735. Mildred Evelyn Keim
736. Ruth Eleanor Keim
737. Robert William Keim
738. William George Baer
739. Virginia Florence Baer
740. William Daniel Falls
741. Elizabeth Marion Falls
742. Ralph Edward Falls
743. Carrie Florence Falls
744. Miriam M. Chesney
745. Ruth May Hanley
746. Mary Jane Hanley
747. Richard Bruce Hanley
748. Inez Underkoffler
749. Carson Underkoffler
750. Wayne Underkoffler
751. Floyd Underkoffler
752. Donald Robert Miller
753. Clinton William Snyder
754. Henry Ford Miller
755. Harold Robert Miller
756. Charles Kohler Eastman
757. Nancy Ann Snyder
758. Blanche Ruth Reigel
759. Calvin Coolidge Reigel
760. Charles Lindberg Reigel
761. Jean Louise Marsh
762. Mae Edna Marsh
763. Leander Rudolph Weiss
764. Arthur William Challinor
765. Robert Schumacher
766. Edward James Doblog
767. Roberta May Doblog
768. Dale Raymond Wean
769. Emmet Jacob Wean
770. Betty Louise Hughes
771. Beverly Joan Hughes
772. Robert Franklin Hughes
773. Richard David Hughes
774. Audrey May Weitzel
775. Barbara Ann Weitzel
776. Dawn Elizabeth Weitzel
777. Charles Irvin Speicher
778. Dorothy Althea Speicher
779. Raymond Kenneth Speicher
780. Betty G. Foreman
781. Dorothy V. Ruppert
782. Richard Percival Jarrett
783. Dorothy Elizabeth Reiman
784. Irene Mae Reiman
785. John Leroy Saylor
786. Charles Gaugler
787. Rebecca Gaugler
788. Ruth Mary Gaugler
789. William Gaugler
790. Betty Ann Hoyer
791. Ella Beulah Hoyer
792. Richard John Hoyer
793. Judith Dawn Gaugler
794. Leroy Paul Beidelman
795. Clair Theodore Beidelman
796. Mary Louise Hartman
797. Lila Marie Hartman
798. Ira Hill Hartman
799. Catherine May Saylor
800. Margaret Mary Saylor
801. Henry Samuel Johnson
802. Richard Allen Johnson
803. Lois Gene Seitzinger
804. Robert Henry Seitzinger
805. Martin Rittenhouse D. Natter
806. Luther Conrad Natter
807. Robert Charles Rudolph
808. Eleanor Rudolph
809. Carl Richard Raber
810. Geraldine Elizabeth Raber
811. William John Raber

812.	Harlen Stanley Fleece	858.	Idella May Bennicoff
813.	Howard J. Wagner	859.	Dean Margaret Bennicoff
814.	James A. Wagner	860.	Mabel Mary Bennicoff
815.	Donald R. Bittenbender	861.	Shirley Ethel Bennicoff
816.	John C. Dudley	862.	Charles Gordon Zieber
817.	Thomas W. Dudley	863.	Daniel Raymond Zieber
818.	Dana Savilla Abel	864.	Carol Elizabeth Yerby
819.	Janice A. Abel	865.	Robert Bruce Yerby
820.	Mary Annie Bailey	866.	James Ronald Nunemacher
821.	Clifford Norman Field	867.	Mary Louise Mengelson
822.	Dian Marie Heckert	868.	Alberta Mae Zimmerman
823.	Richard O. Dudley	869.	Janet Louise Zimmerman
824.	Wayne Youngkin	870.	Bernard Joseph Yeager
825.	Richard Youngkin	871.	Doris May Yeager
826.	Patricia Ellen Rohrbach	872.	Edward Stephen Schlauch
827.	Shirley Fay Rohrbach	873.	Robert Edison Schlauch
828.	William Tobias Rohrbach	874.	Ronald Franklin Schlauch
829.	Arlene May Bernhardt	875.	Gerald Allen Knauf
830.	Elmira Sophia Jarrett	876.	John Thomas Knauf
831.	Richard Lee Mersinger	877.	William Richard Knauf
832.	Lee Franklin Bernhardt	878.	John Henderson Miller
833.	Ardell Eileen Hill	879.	Charlotte Charmane Derry
834.	Constance Charmaine Hill	880.	Gladys Irvina Derry
835.	Helen Marie Kline	881.	Janet Lorraine Derry
836.	Marguerite Ruth Kline	882.	Albert Roye Schropp
837.	Raymond Adam Kline	883.	Pearl Myers Schropp
838.	Yvonne Madelyn Kline	884.	Rosemary Schropp
839.	Audrey Dietz	885.	Daniel Maurer Kepner
840.	Shirley Jean Dietz	886.	Frederick Wertman
841.	Homer S. Dietz	887.	Mary Louise Odenheimer
842.	Albert Harry Stoud	888.	Sylvia Ann Odenheimer
843.	John Allen Stoud	889.	Clarence Kuehn
844.	Paul Frederick Stoud	890.	Ira Kuehn
845.	Robert Leroy Gaugler	891.	James Kuehn
846.	Shirley Mae Gaugler	892.	William Kuehn
847.	Allene Anna Klinger	893.	Albert Thomas Croll
848.	Arlen Talbert Klinger	894.	William Irvin Croll
849.	Richard Marlen Kimmel	895.	Charles William St. Clair
850.	Ruth Elsie Klinger	896.	Donald Ray St. Clair
851.	Treasure Agnes Klinger	897.	Phyllis Marie St. Clair
852.	Barbara Annie Adams	898.	June Dolores Reynolds
853.	Carolyn Anna Adams	899.	Charles Bickel, Jr.
854.	Terrence Lee Adams	900.	Sharley Lynn Mathiot
855.	Betty Virginia Morgan	901.	Shirley Ann Mathiot
856.	Ronald Walter Haas	902.	Glenn Edward Dougherty
857.	Thomas Cary Woodring	903.	James W. Stamm

904.	Dolores Shirley Rebstock	950.	Richard G. Klees
905.	Jacqueline Lucille Rebstock	951.	Ruth Eleanor Hollenbach
906.	Margaret Lorraine Rebstock	952.	Herman John Brodesser
907.	William Earl Rebstock	953.	Carolyn Elizabeth Garber
908.	Patricia Ann Miller	954.	Charles Edward Garber
909.	William Charles Miller	955.	Joseph William Garber
910.	Henrietta Rohrer	956.	John Luther Garber
911.	Edward John Bond	957.	Martin Garber
912.	Jeanette Louise Bond	958.	Richard Garber
913.	Sarah Ann Bond	959.	David Michael Quinn
914.	Clark Frederick Koffke	960.	Linda Adelaide Quinn
915.	Gene Lewis Smith	961.	Walter Eugene Quinn
916.	Glenn Harold Smith	962.	Robert William Wagner
917.	Richard Neal Smith	963.	Ronald Dennis Gehret
918.	Stanley Jonathan Smith	964.	Ralph Franklin Adams
919.	Donald Harold Koch	965.	Jacqueline Mae Amour
920.	Robert J. Koch	966.	Nancy Katherine Amour
921.	Sheldon Ralph Fees	967.	Charlotte L. Kring
922.	Donald Ray Dietrich	968.	Linda L. Kring
923.	Stanley Miller Dietrich	969.	Eugene Edward Smith
924.	Jesse Richard Howell	970.	Norma Lois Smith
925.	Cleta Jane Shellenberger	971.	William Paul Vogol, Jr.
926.	Elane Ada Reber	972.	Judith Eileen Breinig
927.	Pearline Helen Reber	973.	Nancy Louise Breinig
928.	Charles James Powell	974.	Verna Elizabeth Adams
929.	Thomas Alfred Powell	975.	Arthur Sheild Coyle
930.	Edna May Eckenroth	976.	Ronald James Coyle
931.	Francis Raymond Eckenroth	977.	Beverly Jean Bachman
932.	Calvin Robert Lindenmuth	978.	Darlene Judy Bachman
933.	Kathleen S. Styer	979.	Gloria Phyllis Bachman
934.	William Thomas Whitmeyer	980.	Marlene Yvonne Bachman
935.	Gladys Emma Rank	981.	Raymond Harvey Bachman
936.	Catherine May Rollman	982.	Ann Major
937.	Delmer Wayne Rollman	983.	Barbara Major
938.	Irvin George Rollman	984.	Martin Horuath
939.	Ruth Marie Seaman	985.	William Horuath
940.	Barbara Ann Mengel	986.	Janice Loretta Keller
941.	Dale Ronald Mengel	987.	Mervine Alfred Keller
942.	Delma May Mengel	988.	Rosalie Lorraine Keller
943.	Donald Howard Mengel	989.	Irvin Henry Leibold
944.	Lois Alberta Mengel	990.	Vincent Hottle, Jr.
945.	Harry Charles Schanner	991.	Herbert Richard Hoster
946.	Daniel Jacob Sassaman	992.	Kathleen Louise Hoster
947.	Ruth Elizabeth Sassaman	993.	Robert Stanley Leas
948.	Kenneth Edward Sassaman	994.	Sharon Anne Quinn
949.	Randall A. Klees	995.	Charles Lewis Fetter

996. Gloria Lydia Fetter
997. Patricia Ann Fetter
998. Linda Jane Boscoe
999. Arthur C. Henning
1000. Donald Edward Henning
1001. Dorothy Julia Henning
1002. Edithe Ruth Henning
1003. Violet Mae Henning
1004. Dennis Ray Oswald
1005. Dorothy Jane Oswald
1006. Gloria Mae Snyder
1007. Carol Lynn Miller
1008. Fredric K. Leon Hess
1009. Lewis James Hess
1010. Janice M. Karban
1011. Rodney Lee Weiss
1012. Catherine Janet Schimmel
1013. George Francis Schimmel
1014. Patricia Louise Schimmel
1015. Helen Ruth Woodruff
1016. Leonard William Phillips
1017. Michael Allen Allen
1018. Rachel Lois Phillips
1019. Larry Edwin Amy
1020. Leon Benedict Amy
1021. Robert Kenneth Amy
1022. Carol Lou McFarland
1023. Myers McFarland
1024. Linda Pearl Schearer
1025. John Stephen Neweth
1026. Norman M. Comp
1027. Ronald R. Comp
1028. Mary Margaret Phillips
1029. Doris Mae Koehler
1030. Jack Lee Koehler
1031. William Leroy Koehler
1032. Barbara Ann Rompilla
1033. Nicholas Rompilla, Jr.
1034. Paulette Rompilla
1035. Richard Rompilla
1036. Barbara Ann Reitnauer
1037. Irvin Henry Reitnauer
1038. Mark Edwin Reitnauer
1039. Richard Bruce Reitnauer
1040. Clarence Stanley Schaeffer
1041. Elizabeth Jane Schaeffer

1042. Francis Theodore Schaeffer
1043. Russell Lee Schaeffer
1044. Annette Christiana Peischl
1045. Richard John Peischl
1046. Robert Frank Peischl
1047. Victor Charles Peischl
1048. Thomas Michael Peischl
1049. Anna Elizabeth Searles
1050. David Walter Lyali
1051. Raymond Paul Shank
1052. Richard Henry Shank
1053. Sharon May Shank
1054. William Wade Shank
1055. Evelyn Ruth Nikitscher
1056. Ruth Ann Nikitscher
1057. Nancy Jean Shiffert
1058. Barbara Ann Engler
1059. Robert Victor Engler
1060. Sandra Lee Engler
1061. Carl Frederick Wolfe
1062. Elaine Grace Wolfe
1063. Gerald Granville Sorrell
1064. Sandra Lee Santai
1065. Deanna Santai
1066. Joseph Santai
1067. Faye Lucille Ulrich
1068. James Robert Ulrich
1069. Larry Gene Ulrich
1070. Patricia Ann Ulrich
1071. Shirley Jean Ulrich
1072. David Arthur Hess
1073. Laurenette Marie Shaner
1074. Cornelius Ray Ott
1075. Elizabeth Irene Ott
1076. Richard Ferdinand Ott
1077. Barry Lee Koehler
1078. Edward Harry Otter
1079. Alma Matilda Otter
1080. Albert William Wilson, III
1081. Barbara Mary Jane Miller
1082. Ervin Thomas Miller
1083. Harold Allen Miller
1084. Thomas Hassler
1085. Elizabeth Ann Sterner
1086. Florence Barbara Sterner
1087. William Frederick Sterner

1088. Earl Edward Hollenbach
1089. Gene Leslie Hollenbach
1090. Richard Lee Hollenbach
1091. Richard Allen Keiper
1092. Frank Carl Daniel
1093. James Merrick Boyer
1094. Kenton Lewis Boyer
1095. Marian Feibelmann
1096. Pubenza Theresa
    Feibelmann
1097. Grace Mildred Gross
1098. Richard Leon Gross
1099. Gloria Lorraine Eyrich
1100. Anthony Dennis Hoffer
1101. Margo Dorene Allison
1102. Marlene Valerie Allison
1103. Dennis Blythe Allison
1104. Dorothy Elizabeth Breinig
1105. Benjamin Elisa Breinig
1106. Donald Lee Coles
1107. Helen Irene Delp
1108. Joyce Ann Delp
1109. Nelson John Delp
1110. Nancy Jane Gilbert
1111. Jerry Richard Harpel
1112. Amos Levi Breidegam
1113. Dale Bruce Jones
1114. Barbara Ann Lengle
1115. Robert Richard Lengle
1116. John Ruppert
1117. Barry Lee Fry
1118. Beverly Irma Fry
1119. Evelyn Miller
1120. Nancy Miller
1121. James Merrick Boyer
1122. Kenton Lewis Boyer
1123. Donald Elizabeth Lambert
1124. Doris Ann Riopel
1125. Margaret Patricia Heck
1126. Jurate Ziogas
1127. Melvin Charles Lambert
1128. Merrill Lambert
1129. Russell Charles Swartz
1130. Edward John Darcangelo
1131. Adeline Rosalina Reichert
1132. Alice Faye Reichert

1133. Helen Eleanor Reichert
1134. Mae Annette Reichert
1135. Ralph Kenneth Rohn
1136. Warren Harvey Rohn
1137. Carol Ann Arnold
1138. Joan Beverly Mason
1139. Karen Lois Mason
1140. Deene Lesle Arnold
1141. Paul Warnke Arnold
1142. Andrew Zemitis
1143. Uldis Zemitis
1144. Iuars Zemitis
1145. Nancy Elizabeth Sillmann
1146. Ann Marie Faull
1147. James John Faull
1148. William Earl Faull
1149. Emily Pearl Blawn
1150. Mary Ruth Schaeffer
1151. Boyd N. Rapp
1152. Maurice E. Rapp
1153. Dwight Dean Boyer
1154. Patricia Ann Brill
1155. Charles Ernst
1156. Jeanette Ernst
1157. Dorothy Ann Shirey
1158. George Charles Shirey
1159. Gloria Jean Shirey
1160. Larry Kenneth Folk
1161. Roger Cary Folk
1162. Gayle Ann Smith
1163. Sharon Anita Smith
1164. Eugene Walter Zeiber
1165. William Henry Zeiber
1166. Joy Elsie Hundertmark
1167. Don Thomas Freeman
1168. Howard James Geiger
1169. Terry Lee Geiger
1170. Darlene June Kresge
1171. Richard Leroy Kresge
1172. William E. H. Kresge, Jr.
1173. Mantana Bertha
    Bittenbender
1174. Ralph Dinger
1175. George Allen Brown
1176. Leroy Edgar Brown
1177. Richard Lee Huber

1178.	Robert Lee Huber	1224.	Gloria Jean Zeiber
1179.	Jeffrey Forest Bieber	1225.	Beverly Marks
1180.	Sandra Lee L. Bieber	1226.	William Eugene Marks
1181.	Dale Harvey Frey	1227.	Sharon Gallagher
1182.	David Harold Frey	1228.	Robert Paul Hartman
1183.	Lola Ruth Frey	1229.	Sally Jane Weller
1184.	Francis Clare Frey	1230.	Thomas F. Weller
1185.	Russell Harvey Frey	1231.	William D. Weller
1186.	Barry A. Moll	1232.	Martha Louise Dixon
1187.	Carol Ann Adam	1233.	John Marshall Hoffert
1188.	JoAnne Joseph	1234.	Patricia Lynn Hillegas
1189.	Thomas Joseph	1235.	Richard Dale Hillegas
1190.	Joseph Miles Murray	1236.	William Forest Hillegas, Jr.
1191.	Victoria Ann Murray	1237.	Nathan E. Bieber
1192.	Gary William Showers	1238.	Carolyne Jean Hersh
1193.	William Gary Showers	1239.	Evelyne Jean Hersh
1194.	David Charles Geiger	1240.	Earl James Hersh, III
1195.	Charles Lovanus	1241.	Cherie Marie Emory
1196.	Ronald Menges	1242.	Georgann Emory
1197.	George Franklin Klinger	1243.	Georgene Emory
1198.	James Carl Klinger	1244.	Richard Joseph Graham
1199.	Kenneth Lee Klinger	1245.	Duncan Graham, Jr.
1200.	Beverly Ann Hensinger	1246.	Judith Lorraine Bossert
1201.	Gwendolyn Jean Bossons	1247.	Kenneth Eugene Bossert
1202.	Ralph Samuel Bossons	1248.	Linda L. Bossert
1203.	Warren Joseph Bossons	1249.	Larry David Gracely
1204.	Barbara Jean Fisher	1250.	Leon Gerald Gracely
1205.	Margaret Louise Fisher	1251.	Linda Lou Gracely
1206.	Barbara Jean Berringer	1252.	Patricia Ann Schultz
1207.	Sandra Lou Berringer	1253.	Karl Jacob Tewold
1208.	Allen Russell Firestone	1254.	Robert David Van Syckle
1209.	Donald Kenneth Breidegam	1255.	Glenn Harrison Wampole
1210.	Sandra Lee Breidegam	1256.	Judson Brower Wampole
1211.	Joan Dorothy Rowe	1257.	Randall Lee Wampole
1212.	Joann June Dennis	1258.	Michael Allen Brown
1213.	Brenda Lee Dennis	1259.	Glen Ryan Renner
1214.	Robert Allen Lindenmoth	1260.	Marianne May Tosh
1215.	Thomas Gilbert Poe	1261.	Robert Carlton Fisher
1216.	John Elliot Archer	1262.	Stephen Paul Fisher
1217.	Barry Edward Loch	1263.	Earl Eugene Fisher
1218.	Gary Elmer Loch	1264.	Royal James Cole
1219.	Laurence Edwin Loch	1265.	Denice Ann Sterner
1220.	Michael Grant Henry	1266.	Keith Wayne Sterner
1221.	Scott Paul Henry	1267.	Kerry John Sterner
1222.	Nelda Betty Zeiber	1268.	Henry Wallace Watts
1223.	Penelope Irene Zeiber	1269.	Paul W. Weyandt

1270. David Kermit Serfass
1271. Linda Lee Serfass
1272. David Jan Brown
1273. Randy Lynn Brown
1274. Alice Rebecca
1275. John Walter Spangler
1276. Donna Marie Smith
1277. William Frederick Smith
1278. Larry Warren Meckes
1279. Ronald Richard Meckes
1280. Deborah Jane Hemerly
1281. Charles Earl Reppert, Jr.
1282. Sherry Lee Reppert
1283. Susan Carol Reppert
1284. Betty Theresa Hoster
1285. Fayetta Alma Hoster
1286. Leroy Reuben Hoster
1287. Rosalie Faith Hoster
1288. Tyrone Lee Minnich
1289. Thomas Noel Beck Everett
1290. Diana Lee Martin
1291. Marbeth Ann Martin
1292. Joel Eugene Smith
1293. Michael Harding Smith
1294. Rebecca Louise Smith
1295. Ronald Wayne Smith
1296. Jane Ellen Beitler
1297. Raymond William Foulke
1298. Richard Ashley Foulke
1299. Robert Elmer Fretz
1300. William Early Fretz
1301. Alvin Hamm
1302. Richard Leroy Hamm
1303. James Thoms McDonald
1304. Debra Kathryn Steckline
1305. Georgette Alberta Steckline
1306. Linda May Steckline
1307. Charlene Louise Spangler
1308. Fred J. Readinger
1309. Henry R. Readinger, Jr.
1310. Mary Ann Readinger
1311. Diane Grace Swoyer
1312. Joan Darlene Swoyer
1313. Deborah Ann Pascal
1314. Joan Elizabeth Pascal
1315. Mary Jane Pascal
1316. Allen Daniel Potoczny
1317. David Earl Potoczny
1318. Daniel Paul Readinger
1319. Curt Allen Swoyer
1320. Brenda Karin Hole
1321. Chad Terry Hole
1322. Leroy Franklin Ashten
1323. Sandra Elizabeth Smith
1324. Barry Lee Spraut
1325. Glenn Martin Spraut
1326. Matin Luther Spraut, Jr.
1327. Denise Louise Epler
1328. Robert Pierson
1329. Elvin Lamar Sine
1330. Leroy Paul Sine
1331. Olethea Jane Sine
1332. Judy Anne Fisher
1333. Christine Hinkle
1334. Linda Hinkle
1335. Deborah Jean Brown
1336. Judith Lynn Brown
1337. Vincent Curtis Fehr
1338. Lawrence (Larry) Kunkle
1339. John Sponagle
1340. Timothy C. Moll
1341. Robert Martin Schwartz
1342. Wayne Edward Schwartz
1343. Edgar James Pettit
1344. Pearson Leroy Cole
1345. Timothy Allen Cole
1346. Carl Paul Schnibbe
1347. Linda Lorraine Baatz
1348. Dennis Wayne Baatz
1349. Paul Thomas Baatz, Jr.
1350. Scheryl Jean Baatz
1351. Harlen Dane Gehris
1352. Keith Dale Gehris
1353. Kim Lee Gehris
1354. Nevin Lanny Gehris
1355. James Daniel Fritz
1356. William Richard Fritz
1357. Neil Charles Epler
1358. William Harry Hoffman
1359. Bonnie Kathryn Rice
1360. Sandra Lee Dale
1361. Cynthia Lee Hane

1362. Sandra Keiper	1408. Charles William Steffy, Jr.
1363. John William Kline	1409. Lawrence Granville Haydt
1364. Marvin Lee Kline, Jr.	1410. Christine Ann Haydt
1365. Michael John Kline	1411. Barbara Jane Ritter
1366. Thomas Gary Kline	1412. Carolyn May Ritter
1367. Felix Immanuel Ormai	1413. Kermit Antrim Ritter
1368. Beverly Ann Singley	1414. Richard Lee Ritter
1369. Carol Elizabeth Singley	1415. Edward Leonard Chamberlain
1370. John Kelly	1416. Peter Gregory Chamberlain
1371. William Louis Terrey	1417. Toby Calvin Edelman
1372. Kenneth Allen Singley	1418. Betty Pepper Rentschler
1373. James Calvin Weiss	1419. Bonnie Lynn Dunn
1374. William Thomas Weiss	1420. Daniel Claude Cascarino
1375. Barbara Zimmerman	1421. Patrick Pierre Cascarino
1376. Barbara Delp	1422. Robert Paul Sieger
1377. Diane June Gettis	1423. Trudi Genee Swain
1378. Irene Ann Morgan	1424. Linda Marie Kuemmerle
1379. Virginia Ann Seifrit	1425. James Fraley
1380. Robert Lee Washburn	1426. Thomas Fraley
1381. Edwin Bruce Eshleman	1427. Jacqueline Fraley
1382. Ronald Hayden Favinger	1428. Betty Hartranft
1383. Thomas Leroy Favinger	1429. Ronald Hartranft
1384. James Robert Favinger	1430. Carl Rienecker
1385. Bryan George Berlew	1431. Elizabeth Rienecker
1386. Donna Jean Berlew	1432. Theodore A. Geffert
1387. Randy Erwin Berlew	1433. David Richard Wylie
1388. Roxann Helen Berlew	1434. Janet Lee Wylie
1389. Bruce Dana Steever	1435. Katherine Louise Wylie
1390. Joel Atlee Steever	1436. Charlotte Johnson
1391. Randall Preston Snyder	1437. Debra Ann Johnson
1392. Dolores Elizabeth Wagner	1438. Sherry Lee Johnson
1393. Frank George Wagner	1439. Tina Marie Johnson
1394. Raymond Edward Wagner	1440. Joy Christine Rienecker
1395. JoAnne Karen Flint	1441. Barry William Crocker
1396. Frederick J. Mullen	1442. Larry Edward Crocker
1397. Thomas John Mullen	1443. Ricky Blair Sabatine
1398. Linda Ann Spraut	1444. Mark Daniel Fry
1399. Thomas James Spraut	1445. Byron Anthony Fritz
1400. Deborah Ann Ritter	1446. Dean Martin Fritz
1401. Philip Kenneth Ritter	1447. Robert Stephen Bush
1402. Raymond Robert Ritter	1448. Clair Edwin Barry, Jr.
1403. Sylvia Ann Ritter	1449. William Irving Barry
1404. William Lee Ritter	1450. Davie Howard Targett
1405. Roy Dale Weinhold	1451. Tammas Herbert Targett
1406. Daniel Lee Gillmer	1452. Nancy Zelda Fox
1407. David Wilford Gillmer	1453. Walton Henry Fox

1454. Wayne C. Fox, Jr.	1500. Karen Allen
1455. Michael Allen Parnell	1501. Mitzi Allen
1456. Barbara Jean Grube	1502. William Allen
1457. Douglas Lynn Grube	1503. Yolanda Allen
1458. Jed Owen Grube	1504. Cynthia L. Smith
1459. Perry Mitchell Grube	1505. Jack S. Smith
1460. Donald Blake Hatch	1506. Jeffrey A. Smith
1461. John T. Hammond, III	1507. Patricia Smith
1462. Clyde William Madden	1508. Raeleen Smith
1463. Ronald D. Fleck	1509. Nathan V. Deemer
1464. Kathryn Marie Cahoon	1510. Michael Levan
1465. Joseph Allen Cahoon	1511. Thomas Levan
1466. Deborah Ann Sunbury	1512. Daryl P. Leisey
1467. Roy Thomas Sunbury	1513. Allen Scott Rabenold
1468. Arthur William Heckman	1514. Annie Laurie Rabenold
1469. Mary Fox	1515. Gary Deane Rabenold
1470. Michael Thomas Brobst	1516. Kerry Dee Rabenold
1471. Harry M. Auman	1517. Kimberly Ann Rabenold
1472. Lynn C. Nonnemacher	1518. Gerard Wm. Terlesky
1473. David Allen Merkey	1519. Theodore F. Brantley
1474. Dean Christopher Merkey	1520. Oliver Turpin
1475. Thomas J. Merkey, Jr.	1521. Antowyne Charles
1476. Joseph Bosco Farina	1522. Arthur Jones
1477. Donald E. Watts	1523. George P. Smith
1478. Carol Dawn Kratzer	1524. John Thomas Altemos
1479. Diane Marie Bailey	1525. Rene Whales
1480. Donna Dale	1526. Stephen Richard Baer
1481. Kenneth Dale	1527. Roberta May Martin
1482. Linda Dale	1528. Donald Ahart
1483. Richard Dale	1529. George Ahart
1484. Thomas Dale	1530. Arthur Charles Souders
1485 Deborah Dale	1531. Carl Curtis Souders
1486. Charles H. Altemos	1532. Woodrow Luckey Souders
1487. Randy G. Triest	1533. Eddie Zucal
1488. Joann M. Kratzer	1534. Debra Lynn Moore
1489. Martha S. Cobley	1535. David Mertus
1490. Karen Bowling	1536. Mark Cassidy
1491. Donna Bowling	1537. Jeffrey C. Bors
1492. Brian A. Haldeman	1538. Nicholas Santiago
1493. Craig L. Haldeman	1539. Johnny Carter
1494. Palmer G. Haldeman	1540. Carol Sterner
1495. Ricky J. Haldeman	1541. David Shiner, Jr.
1496. Roxann L. Haldeman	1542. Harry Bellangee
1497. Cheryl L. Stehly	1543. James Bellangee
1498. Sadie Young	1544. Leroy Guldner
1499. Jeffrey Allen	1545. Diane G. Fisher

1546.	David Byrd	1593.	Linda G. Cochran
1547.	Kevin Dennis	1594.	Bernadine Stull
1548.	Keith Dennis	1595.	Thomas Bowie
1549.	Diane White	1596.	Russell Breidegam
1550.	Kurt Wolfe	1597.	Judith Boivin
1551.	Marie Byrd	1598.	Donald Mark Fegley
1552.	Shala Darrough	1599.	Frederick Kratzer
1553.	Dorothy McGuire	1600.	Hazel Helmick
1554.	Darryl W. Pettigrew	1601.	Linda DeAngelo
1556.	Donna Bound	1602.	Joseph Klitsch
1557.	Maria Maldanado	1603.	John Klitsch
1558.	Sheldon Jones	1604.	Jerry Klitsch
1559.	Charles Enrique Alvarez	1605.	John Hyneman
1560.	Kathy Ann Carter	1606.	David Fields
1561.	Leroy Ronald Teflie	1607.	Charles Fields
1562.	Frank Lynn Yost	1608.	Kenneth Jones
1563.	Joseph Powell	1609.	William Weitzmann
1564.	Thomas P. Kahler	1610.	Edward Brown
1565.	James Joseph Richmond	1611.	Andrew Carey
1566.	Michael Bitting	1612.	Kerry Knarr
1567.	Rodney Allen Batchler	1613.	Kittie Charleville
1568.	George Dawson	1614.	Susan Powers
1569.	Sandra Pagan	1615.	Pamela Ann Wells
1570.	Randall Dale Everitt	1616.	Thomas Michael Watts
1571.	Karen Kerns	1617.	William Teal
1572.	Marguerita Lopez	1618.	German Rivera
1573.	Ernesta Lee Copeland		
1574.	Denise Cantagallo		
1575.	Edward Rivera		
1576.	John Joseph Coppie		
1577.	Lorraine Chapman		
1578.	Shelly Lee Leatherman		
1579.	Sherry Lynn Leatherman		
1580.	Daniel Raymond Kline		
1581.	Thomas Coppie		
1582.	Joseph Page		
1583.	James Small		
1584.	Patricia Brigham		
1585.	Janice Erney		
1586.	Lois Erney		
1587.	Donald Jacobs		
1588.	Jerry M. McCarraher		
1589.	Henry Long		
1590.	Robin Stephens		
1591.	Victoria Dever		
1592.	Judy Oliver		

To comfort and to bless,

To find a balm for woe,
To tend the lone
and fatherless,

Is angels work below.

BIBLIOGRAPHY

Cowen, Dick, *Papa Raker's Dream:* Allentown, PA; The Good
     Shepherd Home, 1988
Youcha, Geraldine, *Minding the Children:*New York,
     Scribner, 1995
The Lutheran Home at Topton publications
     *Charter, By-Laws and Regulations of the Lutheran
     Orphans' Home:* Reading, PA, 1915
     Twenty-Fifth Anniversary of the Lutheran Orphans' Home:
     Topton, PA, 1922
     *Lutheran Orphans' Home, 1897-1937; Fortieth Anniversary
     of the Lutheran Orphans' Home:* Topton, PA, 1937
     *Providing For Them: A History of the Lutheran Home of
     Topton:*Topton, PA, 1972

ABOUT THE AUTHOR

David A. Miller, II's first writing assignments
were as a 'summer reporter' during his years
at Muhlenberg College, working for the
<u>Allentown Morning Call</u> newspaper, founded
by his grandfather, David A. Miller.

While Miller has written and edited many
newsletters and articles as President
of Miller Marketing since 1977,
A Gift of Love is his first full-length book.
Another proud accomplishment was the
Lutheran World Hunger 'African Drought'
campaign, which saw his materials in every
Lutheran church in North America.

He has worked on projects for
The Lutheran Home at Topton since 1980
and looks forward to the updating of this
volume for the 125th anniversary!